CW00925389

This h   to b   on or before

S.I.M.P. Research Monograph No. 5

Children Living
in Long-stay Hospitals

MAUREEN OSWIN

Foreword by Jack Tizard

1978

Spastics International Medical Publications

LONDON: William Heinemann Medical Books Ltd.

PHILADELPHIA: J. B. Lippincott Co.

ISBN 0 433 24250 7

Printed in England at THE LAVENHAM PRESS LTD., Lavenham, Suffolk

/393

Contents

ACKNOWLEDGEMENTS

Acknowledgements are due to Peter Moss of the Thomas Coram Research Unit, who had the initial idea that I should undertake a study of children in hospital, and to James Loring, Director of The Spastics Society, who very generously agreed that the Society should finance the project.

During the final writing up of the study, I was very kindly given a short period of financial support by the Chase Charity and by groups of parents of mentally handicapped children in south-east England—I must record my thanks for that help, which was organised by Mr. C. C. Younger of the Chase Charity and by Lesley Marks and Chris Francis of the National Society for Mentally Handicapped Children.

Special thanks are due to the staff of the hospitals I visited, who, although aware that I was engaged on a study which was likely to be critical of hospital services, never failed to make me welcome and always let me obtain an honest picture of what was happening to the children. In the honesty of the staff and their willingness to risk criticism there lies much hope for future better services for children in long-stay hospitals.

I also thank Dr. Chris Kiernan of the Thomas Coram Research Unit, and Professor Peter Mittler of the Hester Adrian Research Centre, who very kindly read the final manuscript and gave time for helpful discussion on various points.

Finally, I thank Professor Jack Tizard, Director of the Thomas Coram Research Unit, whose commitment to the improvement of services for handicapped children has long been an inspiration to all who work in this field. He gave invaluable advice and personal encouragement throughout the time I was working on this study, and I am glad to have this opportunity to express my gratitude.

The extracts from *Better Services for the Mentally Handicapped* (Cmnd. 4683), *Educating Mentally Handicapped Children* (DES Pamphlet No. 60) and *Fit for the Future* (Cmnd. 6684) are reprinted with the permission of the Controller of Her Majesty's Stationery Office.

Some of the references to Sally, Bob, Tom and Mary on pages 101, 103 and 142-145 (respectively) previously appeared in a paper entitled 'Physically handicapped children in long-stay hospitals', given by the author at the International Cerebral Palsy Society Conference, Oxford, 1977, and subsequently published in *Child: Care, Health and Development*, (1977), 3, 349-355.

Foreword

JACK TIZARD

Children who are *profoundly* retarded constitute only a small proportion of those whom we call mentally handicapped. But they present severe and intractable problems of management and care. The gravity of their handicaps is such that, even with the most skilled nursing and the most assiduous educational treatment, they make little progress. And since the brain damage from which they suffer is diffuse, severe and irreversible, advances in treatment cannot promise too much in the way of remediation. In consequence, even the great physicians, educators and psychologists of the past — Séguin, Decroly, Binet, Montessori — tended to neglect the profoundly retarded, to blot them from consciousness as it were, since their presence was an affront to their vision of the educability of the human intelligence. Moreover, our predecessors could claim a certain justification for this neglect, since nearly all profoundly retarded children died in infancy or early childhood. Indeed, they were called 'idiots' — persons who were not really part of humanity, but rather apart from it. Like unbaptised children in an earlier Christian age, they could scarcely be said to exist.

Circumstances have changed, and with them attitudes. Advances in medicine have reduced the numbers of multiply handicapped children who are born, yet these same advances have increased their life-span. So although the incidence at birth has decreased, the prevalence of profound mental retardation at later ages has increased. How best to care for the multiply handicapped, and how to enable them to live lives that are as rich and meaningful as possible, has in consequence become not merely an ethical, psychological and nursing problem affecting only a few, but also a social problem affecting substantial numbers of people.

Maureen Oswin brings to the study of profoundly retarded children in mental handicap hospitals a wealth of knowledge and experience derived from years of teaching severely disabled children. She is a good observer, and she has a conscience which is informed by knowledge as well as by compassion. Over a period of 18 months she spent nearly all her time in the wards of eight mental handicap hospitals in order to prepare the material for this book, and the descriptions she gives of what she experienced have the ring of truth. However, her account is not just another 'exposure' of the shortcomings of our hospitals. She is aware of the shortcomings of course, and she describes them objectively; but she is aware too of the enormous problems which the

v

hard-pressed nursing staff meet in their daily life, and of their lack of support from the specialists, the consultants and the public, who should provide it. The very many practical suggestions for improvement which she makes give the book a special character: it should be read by all who are concerned with the mentally handicapped.

Fortunately, recent advances in the study of mental handicap do begin to suggest more fruitful ways of helping children than those usually employed today. Behaviour modification programmes can, in principle, offer very much more than the recipes being tried out in the hospitals studied by Miss Oswin; and as she herself shows, close observation of individual children indicates that much of their apparently disordered or random behaviour is meaningful and purposeful once it is seen in context. But if we are to advance our knowledge and, more important, to improve our practice, it is to nurses and teachers rather than doctors, psychologists or therapists, that we must turn. To increase staffing ratios and to enable primary-care staff to improve their technical skills are the two most urgent needs facing our residential services. Only when we meet these needs will we be able to provide an environment which will enable the most severely handicapped children to fulfil their potential and live more meaningful lives.

In an account of this sort, it is always difficult to make the children 'come alive'. It is too easy to describe them simply in terms of what they cannot do, and to see life in the ward just as a series of 'problems'. Because Miss Oswin writes vividly and well, however, the children do come alive in the pages of this text. But to get a rounded picture of what it's really like on these wards, I recommend the reader to turn first to Appendix 1, which could well have formed the opening chapter to the book. It would be a pity if placing *Scenes from Ward 7* in an appendix (in order not to have the book labelled as 'sensational') should lead people to skip it. For the description given is both powerful and depressing. It brings out very clearly the issues with which the rest of the book is concerned, and it reveals how far we are from providing in our long-stay hospitals an environment fit for children to live in, and for staff to work in.

Introduction

Approximately four children in every thousand who reach adolescence are severely mentally handicapped. Some of these children may also have other disabilities such as cerebral palsy, spina bifida, deafness, blindness or partial sight, hydrocephalus, microcephalus or bone malformations. They may also be speechless, incontinent, non-ambulant, and need help with feeding, washing and dressing.

Multiply handicapped children present very grave problems to their families and to other people who care for them. The Department of Health and Social Security has frequently stated that it is necessary for these children to remain permanently in hospital because they "require treatment or training under specialist medical supervision or constant nursing care"[1]. There is general agreement on this point among hospital consultants and administrators of local authority social service departments, because it is thought that only a hospital can provide the services required by children with severe multiple handicaps.

The 1970 census of mentally handicapped patients in hospital in England and Wales[2] showed that there were 10,915 severely mentally handicapped children aged 19 years and younger living in mental handicap hospitals, and 6093 of these were aged from under five years up to 15 years. The census gave the following details about the handicaps of the 10,915 children: 3123 were non-ambulant, 5540 were severely incontinent, 5969 needed much help with feeding, washing or dressing, 834 had severe sight defects (blind or almost blind), 368 had severe hearing defects (deaf or almost deaf) and 5410 had a severe speech defect (never spoke).

Since 1968 the number of children up to 15 years of age in mental handicap hospitals has actually been declining at an annual rate of approximately 6 per cent. Between 1973 and 1974 the rate had increased to 9 per cent, and the decline was most marked for younger children: for those under five years of age the decrease was 12.1 per cent, for those from five to nine years it was 13.4 per cent, and for those from 10 to 14 years it was 6 per cent. The number of children in mental handicap hospitals in 1974 was estimated to be approximately 4500[3].

In Britain the cost of accommodating a patient in a mental handicap hospital is approximately £70 a week (DHSS figure for 1976-77; personal communication, January 1978).

1. Department of Health and Social Security (1971) *Better Services for the Mentally Handicapped*. Cmnd. 4683. London: H.M.S.O. para. 180.
2. Department of Health and Social Security (1972) *Statistical and Research Report Series No. 3*. London: H.M.S.O. Table MH19 (patients in hospital less than one month at time of census are excluded).
3. Department of Health and Social Security (1977) *Mentally Handicapped Children: a Plan for Action*. National Development Group pamphlet No. 2. London: H.M.S.O. p. 24.

The decline in the number of children living permanently in hospitals for the mentally handicapped reflects the efforts being made to keep mentally handicapped children in the community for as long as possible by providing more children's Homes, more short-term care rather than permanent hospital admission, more support for families, and by exploring other forms of care, such as fostering. However, community care tends to be more easily available for the less-handicapped children, while the more severely handicapped (especially those with behaviour problems or physical disabilities) are still being admitted to long-stay hospitals.

The present study

Early in 1975 it was agreed by the Department of Health and Social Security and the Department of Education and Science that I should make a study of the care being given to some of the most severely handicapped children living in hospitals for the mentally handicapped, in order to see how their needs were being met. The Spastics Society generously financed the Study, and I was based at the Thomas Coram Research Unit, University of London Institute of Education, under the direction of Professor Jack Tizard.

Eight hospitals in different parts of the country were chosen for the study, the aim being to have a mixture of older and newer hospitals in order to have as representative a sample as possible. The senior staff in the hospitals gave me permission to look at the services they were providing for multiply handicapped children, and I spent between four and nine weeks in each hospital. Without exception, I was received with great kindness in every hospital, and the nursing staff were particularly helpful. No questionnaires were used, nor were the staff formally interviewed. Information was obtained by my making continuous observations during approximately 40 periods of 12-14 hours, 50 periods of 6-8 hours and 50 periods of 4-5 hours. These observation periods were interspersed by my working alongside staff in the routine care of the children. I accompanied the children to hospital school and therapy, went on outings with them, and took part in ward parties and swimming. I met some of the children's parents, hospital volunteers, and all disciplines of staff who were concerned with the multiply handicapped children, and was invited to case conferences and staff meetings. I also met members of Community Health Councils, Area Health Authorities and Regional Health Authorities, and local voluntary organisations connected with handicapped children. I visited local special day-schools, children's Homes, assessment centres and day nurseries, and made contact with local authority social service departments regarding present and future services for multiply handicapped children.

After 18 months of observations and visits it was possible to build up a general picture of the services being offered to multiply handicapped children living in hospitals for the mentally handicapped, and to understand some of the problems facing the staff. This report attempts to describe the situation of the children, the staff and the families.

CHAPTER 1

The Children: Their Circumstances and Their Needs

All 223 children observed in this study live in 'special-care' wards, a term here used to define wards which accommodate only children with multiple physical, mental and sensory handicaps.

I refer throughout this report to 'the children', although their ages ranged up to 29 years. The numbers of children in the various age-groups were: under five years (16); five to 10 years (57); 11 to 16 years (106); 17 to 21 years (32); and 22 to 29 years (12). The 12 adults (22 to 29 years) lived in children's wards because there was no room for them in adult wards. The placement of young multiply handicapped adults, who have already spent their childhood in children's special-care wards, is becoming a major problem in mental handicap hospitals because of the shortage of places for them in adult special-care wards. In some children's wards the age-range is now as wide as from two to 30 years.

Length of stay in hospital

Six of the 223 children had been admitted to hospital for periods of between two and four weeks short-term care, as a means of supporting their families. Three others had been admitted for assessment and remained in hospital for between four and eight weeks. (These nine children are included in the total number observed in the study since they comprised part of the ward populations at the time.)

The other 214 children were permanent long-stay patients. Some went home for occasional week-ends or holidays, and six, who had a regular arrangement to spend most week-ends at home, were referred to by staff as 'boarders'. Some of the long-stay children were visited very regularly but did not go home, while others had very little contact with their families (see Chapter 2 for information about family links).

The 214 long-stay children had been living in hospital for between one and 27 years. Some had lived in other hospitals for several years before being admitted to their present hospital. The children's ages at admission were as follows: under two years (28); between two and five years (64); six and 10 years (87); 11 and 16 years (10); and over 17 years (2). For 23 children the age at admission was unknown*. The number of years they had spent in hospital were: one to five years (71); six to 10 years (59); 11 to 15 years (50); 16 to 19 years (9); and more than 20 years (2). Again, in 23 cases the number of years spent in hospital was unknown*.

*Records for these 23 children were not available or were incomplete.

1

Diagnosed conditions

The case-notes for 180 of the children broadly described them as 'brain damaged' or 'spastic'. The damage had resulted from birth injury, microcephaly, illness in infancy (*i.e.* encephalitis or meningitis), or from unknown causes.

More specific diagnoses had been made for another 25 children, including hydrocephalus (10), spina bifida (4), rubella infection (4), road accidents (3), congenital syphilis (1) and epiloia (1). The remaining two were described as 'battered babies', and their parents had served prison sentences for the assaults.

Of the remaining 18 children, nine had Down's syndrome and nine had other rare conditions or clinical syndromes.

Additional physical conditions affecting some of the children were: epilepsy (138), asthma (2), heart disease (2) and chronic skin-disease (ringworm and eczema) (2).

Multiple disabilities affecting independence

Of the 223 children, 212 were unable to dress or wash themselves, 197 were incontinent, 196 were unable to speak, 189 were non-ambulant, 170 did not feed themselves, 134 were fed on mashed food because of chewing or swallowing difficulties, 66 could not grasp objects in their hands, and 33 were known to be blind.

Mobility. Children were considered to be ambulant if they could walk without the help of another person. Bottom-shuffling, rolling, crawling or manoeuvring a wheelchair were classified as non-ambulant. Only 34 of the children were able to walk without help; another 25 were able to bottom-shuffle, roll or crawl, and 10 could manoeuvre a wheelchair. Thus only 69 of the 223 children had some mobility; the other 154 were completely immobile.

Speech. The 27 children who could speak were unable to hold a conversation, their speech consisting mainly of repeating single words, questions or 'catch-phrases'. None of the 223 children used gesture as a means of communication, the apparent reason being not that the children were physically or mentally incapable of learning meaningful gestures, but that the hospital staff (teachers, nurses, doctors and therapists) were uninformed about how systems of 'signing' might help such severely multiply handicapped children to communicate. Many of the children might have been able to communicate by gesture had the staff known how to teach them to do so (see also pp. 24-26).

Sensory handicap. It was not possible to get accurate figures for the incidence of blindness, partial sight or deafness. The available information was unreliable because staff disagreed among themselves about how much a child could see or hear; because the majority of the children had not been tested for sensory handicaps; and because the information in the case-notes often was contradictory.

Only one child in the study regularly wore glasses, and he was a fairly able

2

21-year-old with cerebral palsy. Three other children were known to have been issued with glasses but did not wear them, and one child wore a hearing-aid (only during school hours).

Reasons for permanent admission to hospital

Although it was assumed that multiply handicapped children live in hospitals because they need continuous medical and nursing care, the circumstances of admission of the children in this study indicate that in fact long-term admission is caused by one or more of the following: lack of support for parents; existing problems within the family; lack of parental home; or lack of residential accommodation within the community.

Lack of support for parents. The lack of support for the parents of multiply handicapped children has several inter-related factors. There is a lack of *practical* support within the community: for example, the parents find it difficult to get aids in the house, guidance on physical care, or advice on the management of feeding problems. Parents may also have had difficulty in forming a relationship with their handicapped child, which may have begun with the separation of mother and baby in the early weeks of life and never have become satisfactorily resolved because of the lack of parental counselling and community support. Further lack of support occurs when professional opinion persuades parents that hospital is 'the best place' for severely incapacitated children. A major factor too is the intense physical and emotional strain suffered by parents who have a multiply handicapped child at home. They may become physically exhausted by the lifting and carrying as the child grows, and by their sleep being interrupted by the child's fretful nights. Some parents of handicapped children never have a holiday, or even an evening out together. They may be alarmed by the child's feeding problems or by the likelihood of his having a major fit, and they may be unhappy because they feel that they do not give their other children enough attention. They may also have pressure put on them by in-laws who advise them to "put him away".

Existing problems within the family. Existing family problems are exacerbated by having a multiply handicapped child living at home. Such problems include inadequate or unsuitable housing, being a single parent, there already being a large family, parental psychiatric or physical illness, poverty, or there already being a handicapped child in the family.

Lack of parental home. This can occur because of death, divorce or separation of the parents, because the child has only a single parent who relinquished him at birth, because the parents are in H.M. Forces and have no settled home, or because the parents have emigrated.

Lack of residential accommodation within the community. Some parents, although at first opposed to long-stay hospital care for their children, eventually find that they have to accept it because no alternative form of care is available. Other children 'drift' into long-stay care because they have already had several periods of short-term care in hospital. None of the eight local authorities in this study offered residential places for children with severe multiple handicaps: they all recommended long-stay hospital admission. Only one local authority had plans to provide residential accommodation for non-ambulant multiply handicapped children: five places will be provided in a complex of three small homes being built between 1976 and 1982 to accommodate a total of 15 mentally handicapped children.

The following stories, which are typical ones, describe how four children became permanently hospitalised.

Bertha

In 1953, when she was 18 months old, Bertha was examined and classified as 'an imbecile', under the 1913 Mental Deficiency Act. She was spastic and partially sighted. Although she was still only a baby, her parents were advised to make application for her institutional care. The necessary petitions were made, according to the 1913 Act, then the Order for Detention was made out, authorising 'the defective's detention'. This Order eventually admitted Bertha to a mental handicap hospital at the age of four.

She was described in her Reception Order as 'an epileptic idiot'. After a year in that first hospital she was transferred to another one: on transfer, the section of her hospital notes headed 'Programme of Treatment and Training' merely advised 'care only'. There was no thought of education or therapy. Like all the other multiply handicapped children in her ward, she was kept in a cot all the time: the ward was called 'the cot and chair ward'.

Bertha shouted a great deal, and her nursing notes over the next five years make constant reference to her noisiness and to the various sedatives used in attempts to quieten her. Up to the age of nine, her daily ward-notes had such entries as 'still noisy' and 'as noisy as ever'. At 10 years the notes stated 'Valium makes her better' and 'this is the first drug to control her noisiness, which has been a menace for years'. At this age there was also a brief note that she 'pulled herself up in her cot', but there was no comment on this possibly being a sign of progress.

Bertha is now 24 years old and is still in the children's special-care ward at the hospital where she had been living for the last 19 years. Today, however, Bertha and the other multiply handicapped children and young adults in her ward are not kept in cots all the time. They are all got up, and a few have physiotherapy and education.

The legal processes for admission to mental handicap hospitals have changed over the years, and a spastic child would not now be described as a defective needing detention, but the basic reasons for admittance remain unchanged: that multiply handicapped children require a form of sheltered residential care, and a long-stay hospital for the mentally handicapped usually is the only type of residential care available.

Lewis

Thirteen-year-old Lewis is cerebral-palsied, epileptic, partially sighted, non-ambulant, incontinent and speechless. He relies on the ward staff for all his physical care. He was admitted to a mental handicap hospital at three years of age because of his family's grave housing problems — only two rooms for a very large family. The application for Lewis's permanent hospital admission was made by the County's Medical Officer of Health, who described him as 'a cot case'. That was in 1966. Today Lewis sits in a wheelchair, attends hospital school and is regularly visited by his family.

Jack

Now 11 years old, Jack was only one year old when a paediatrician wrote to the County Medical Officer of Health that 'owing to the hopeless future for this child, I think that if he could be accepted in — — — — Hospital it would be absolutely the right decision'. Within eight months of that letter being written, Jack was admitted permanently to a hospital for the mentally handicapped. Since his admission his parents have been divorced and no longer visit him, but his grandparents keep good contact.

He can bottom-shuffle about the room and can stand if supported. He is incontinent, speechless and needs help with feeding, but is expected to make progress. He attends the hospital school, has physiotherapy, goes swimming in the hospital pool and is learning to ride a tricycle.

Clive

Twelve-year-old Clive's mental and physical disabilities were caused by spina bifida. He is non-ambulant, incontinent and mentally retarded, but can feed himself and help a little when being dressed. He can manoeuvre his wheelchair around the room and can say a few words. He attends the hospital school.

Clive had had operations shortly after birth to correct his spina bifida, and had then remained in the general hospital for a year because his mother felt unable to accept him. He was discharged home at the age of one year, but soon afterwards his mother was suspected of neglecting him and he was re-admitted to the general hospital, after which he was officially taken into care. From the age of four to seven years Clive was fostered, but his foster-parents were elderly, and by the time he was seven years old he had become too heavy for them to lift. New foster-parents could not be found, so Clive was admitted to the mental handicap hospital where he has now been living for the last five years. His parents are now divorced: his mother does not visit him but his father maintains good contact.

The children's needs

These needs might be divided broadly into four categories: medical, paramedical and education, nursing, and residential care.

Medical needs

(1) Diagnosis of disability.

(2) Special treatment (for some children): drugs (for epilepsy); orthopaedic correction of deformities; surgical correction of eye defects; cosmetic correction (*i.e.* plastic surgery for grave facial deformities); and psychiatric help for emotional disturbances.

(3) Supervision of general health care (as for ordinary children); treatment of common childhood illnesses, accidents, dietary problems, skin diseases; dental care; glasses and hearing-aids if necessary; and referral to other specialists as required.

Paramedical and educational needs

Physiotherapy for supervision of movement, position, aids, furniture, wheelchairs, calipers, boots, and for assisting to become more independent.

Speech therapy, especially when there are early feeding problems. The grave handicaps of these children make it necessary to explore various means of communication, by all disciplines of staff, and then some experimentation to find the best method for each individual child.

Occupational therapy to assist independence, for example in learning to hold a cup, spoon or flannel and sponge, to put on shoes or pull on socks, to lift arms to help with dressing. Occupational therapists can advise on how to make use of any ability, however meagre.

Psychological advice on helping the children to become more independent, for example through carefully worked-out programmes of individual teaching, and for the correction or prevention of behaviour disorders.

Education covers the needs to play and to communicate; special educational help for children who are blind, deaf, partially sighted or who have physical disabilities (*e.g.* equipment, aids, teaching methods). Referral to other special educational centres (perhaps schools outside the hospital) if necessary.

Nursing needs

These will be required for some, but not all, of the children: drugs; medicines; occasional enemas; special diets; care during and after major epileptic attacks; prevention of sores when children are emaciated or very physically deformed; attending to children with colostomies; caring for children with severe handicaps resulting from spina bifida; and care of children after operations or during illnesses.

Residential care needs

Routine physical care: supervision of clothes; food, cleanliness; attention in the lavatory; safety; care during minor illnesses; general health care, as for ordinary children living away from home.

Mothering*: essential for all children in residential care, whether disabled or not.

---

*'Mothering', as used in this study, does not imply care which can only be given by a woman; it is used in the sense of affectionate individual care being given by a man or woman. The word parenting was considered, but discarded in favour of the more meaningful word mothering.

Family contact: important for all children in residential care, whether disabled or not.

Personal possessions: essential for all children in residential care, whether disabled or not.

Play: essential for all children in residential care, whether disabled or not.

Outings: essential for all children in residential care, whether disabled or not.

The majority of the needs listed above are no different from those of ordinary children in residential care or in the family home. In order to meet these needs of multiply handicapped children in residential care, there must be adequate numbers of care staff, who need to be supported in a practical way by specialist staff; there has to be inter-disciplinary co-operation.

The extent to which the children's needs are being satisfied will be seen in the following chapters.

CHAPTER 2

Families

Over the last 10 years, and especially since the publication in 1972 of the DHSS leaflet on the subject[4], attention has been given to the possibility that children in long-stay hospitals may be abandoned by their parents.

Reliable information about family contacts was obtainable for 185 of the 214 long-stay children in this study. 34 had no family contact at all, 28 were very infrequently visited (less than once a year), 12 had infrequent visits (not more than two or three times a year), and the remaining 111 had frequent visits (regularly once a month, every week, or in some cases as often as three or four times a week).

These figures might be taken to indicate that the families of one-fifth of the long-stay children care little about what happens to them. However, the emotive word 'abandonment' can be misused to condemn non-visiting parents, while diverting attention from the shortcomings of social provision for handicapped children, which all too often means that long-stay hospital care is the only form of help available to the families. Within the group of so-called 'abandoned' children, there are families who themselves have been abandoned by their local health authorities, the medical profession and the local authority social service departments.

A social policy which favours the admission of children to long-stay hospitals rather than providing support in the family home (combined, if necessary, with residential care in homes near the family's own home) immediately puts the children at risk of losing contact with their families. For example, Bay Hospital* was opened as an 'asylum' in 1913, and in 1975 had 1400 mentally handicapped people living in it. It is situated in remote countryside, 12 miles from the nearest town. It took me 20 minutes to walk up the long drive from the road to the hospital. Ward 2, one of the wards for severely handicapped children, was opened in 1962, and by 1975 there were 26 children living there. Five of these children had no family contact at all, three had infrequent visits (two very infrequent) and 18 were visited frequently. The eight children who had little or no contact with their families were aged between nine and 16 years; their ages when admitted for long-term care were three years (1), two years (3), one year (3) and less than one year (1).

When children are taken into an institution for long-term care at such young ages, it can be argued that they have never really belonged to their families and that therefore it is incorrect to describe them as abandoned. Some

4. Department of Health and Social Security (1972) *Children in Hospital: Maintenance of Family Links and Prevention of Abandonment*. London: H.M.S.O.
*'Bay' Hospital is a pseudonym, as are the names used for the other hospitals in this study.

8

so-called 'abandoned' children have never actually been home to their families; on the advice of doctors who sincerely believe that severely handicapped children should be admitted to hospital for long-term care, they have remained in general or children's hospitals after their birth and have later been transferred to mental handicap hospitals. Their parents have never had the opportunity of making a bond with them.

Emily

Thirteen-year-old Emily was in this situation. She had been born with congenital facial and limb deformities, and at one year of age she was sent to a long-stay hospital for physically handicapped children. Her parents were not encouraged to have anything to do with her. She remained in the children's hospital for eight years and was then transferred to a long-stay hospital for the mentally handicapped. She was there for six months and was then transferred again to a new mental handicap hospital, where she has remained ever since.

When Emily was nine years old, the paediatrician at the children's hospital where she was living wrote to the consultant of the mental handicap hospital to which she was being transferred: he said 'I think, quite understandably, the mother has been quite unable to accept this baby and indeed was under the care of psychiatrists with severe mental symptoms as the result of having given birth to this child. It was thought wiser to make a complete break and in fact we have had no connection with the parents throughout the time that the child has been here (eight years) and I think there is some doubt whether indeed they live at the address we have been giving you.'

Emily was disfigured by a rare syndrome, and it would have required sensitive long-term support to console her parents and help them to make a relationship with their little girl, which they might have done even though she had remained in hospital. But they did not receive that support, and the negative attitudes of the medical profession encouraged them to relinquish her. It is possible that the effects of never knowing their child and thinking that they had given birth to a child who had to be hidden, were more harmful to the parents than if they had tried to build up a relationship with her and perhaps failed.

Abandonment, in the sense of *wilfully* losing contact with the child, occurs very rarely. If parents do lose contact with their child in hospital, the causes are likely to be: (1) the philosophy of admission to long-term care (*i.e.* 'putting away', as occurred to Emily); (2) travel difficulties; or (3) family problems (illness, death, poverty, single-parent families, large families).

Occasionally some tragic incident results in a child being totally without family contact. For example, when Freda was a baby her mother was in despair at the severity of her handicaps, so she decided to gas herself and Freda together. She died, but Freda survived. The mother's death made Freda's father psychiatrically disturbed, and Freda has now been living in a long-stay hospital for 10 years and has no family contact.

9

Parents feel a tremendous sense of loss when they finally have to let their children go into long-stay hospitals, and it seems that the purely physical relief of having their child cared for by other people does little to assuage the gap they feel when they know the child has left home for good; nor does physical relief ease the parents' sense of having failed their child because they can no longer care for him at home. Too little account is taken of the fact that parents may 'mourn' for their child in a long-stay hospital and find it emotionally difficult to visit him. Other parents cease to visit because they are distressed at seeing the other severely handicapped children, or they feel unwelcome in the ward and are not sure of their rôle in relation to their child because they are no longer responsible for his care. Parents of children in long-stay hospitals could be supported by more counselling from hospital staff to deal with the many emotional problems of having a child living in an institution.

It is significant that, of the eight hospitals in this study, Pine was the one with the most positive contact with parents. This hospital accommodated 290 mentally handicapped residents. It had been built in 1970 and was easy to reach by public transport. The wards were bright and pleasant. The staff made a point of welcoming parents, and each ward had a Parents' Association. Some parents visited several times a week; they put their own children to bed and sat down afterwards to have coffee with the staff. Ward 10 of this hospital accommodated 17 multiply handicapped children and one short-stay child. The visiting patterns for the long-stay children were: one child had no contact at all with his family; one had very infrequent visits (three visits in five years); three had infrequent visits (two to three times a year); and 12 had regular and frequent visits.

The hospital with the next best contact with parents was Willows (200 patients). It had recently been rebuilt on its old site near the centre of a small market town, and the wards were bright and attractive. Since its rebuilding, Willows had developed a new policy of encouraging parent involvement in the wards, and each ward had an active Parents' Group. The special-care ward accommodated 20 long-stay multiply handicapped children and young adults, aged between two and 29 years. 13 of the children were in very close contact with their families, five had no contact at all, and two had very infrequent visits. It is significant that the five young people who had no contact with their families had all been in hospital for at least 13 years, and had all been admitted before the age of six, during a time when the hospital's policy had not been to encourage parental involvement.

The amounts of parental involvement at both Pine and Willows hospitals indicate that families find it easier to maintain links with their children if residential care is offered locally, in pleasant surroundings, and with welcoming staff.

Reclaiming families

In Willows Hospital, attempts were being made to reclaim families who had lost touch, or who were maintaining only tenuous links with the children.

For example, 17-year-old George had been in hospital for 13 years. His parents had moved away from the district and he had received no visits for five years. The doctors at Willows Hospital were writing to George's parents, explaining how George was getting on and describing some of his abilities (*e.g.* he could now say a few words and liked playing with a ball). It was hoped that in this way George's parents might be encouraged to renew their links with him.

Relationship between staff and families

Misunderstandings occur because parents and staff suspect each other of being critical. Staff often think that parents criticise the care given to their children, and parents think that staff criticise them for having 'dumped' their children. In Ash Hospital, a parent said: "I know the staff think I've dumped my child. They don't say anything to my face, but they give me disapproving looks". The staff of Ash Hospital's special-care ward were noticeably unsympathetic towards parents, making such remarks as:

"They're greedy for what they can get out of the state."
"They don't want to know, they've dumped him."
"They criticise us for not caring for him properly, but they won't look after him themselves."
"Parents don't understand staff problems, we have 24 children to look after, not just one."
"Peg's mother has a nice time when she comes. She gets her fare paid by the social work department, she brings all the other kids, and they enjoy a picnic in the grounds, like a bloody Sunday-school outing."
"They spoil the kids, bringing them great bags of sweets and food."
"Parents are no help to us."

These remarks were often provoked by under-staffing and the pressure of work in that ward. 13 of the 24 children in this ward had very infrequent visits from their families, one had no contact at all, and two had infrequent contact. Only eight children were visited regularly. These visiting patterns were in marked contrast to those in Willows and Pine hospitals, where parents were made welcome and where the staff often said: "We're here to help parents".

If parents were popular with ward staff, it was generally due to one or more of the following reasons:
(1) Visiting regularly.
(2) Helping with tasks to do with their own child's care (*e.g.* feeding and washing).
(3) 'Accepting' their child, and not expecting the staff to 'cure' him.
(4) Not having a critical attitude towards the staff.
(5) Still continuing to visit, in spite of poverty or grave family problems.
(6) Being grateful for what the staff did for their child.
Unpopularity appeared to be due to:
(1) Never visiting, although within travelling distance.
(2) Treating nurses like servants.

(3) Expecting unrealistic progress (this was said by staff to be 'not accepting' their child's disabilities).

(4) Criticising hospital care.

(5) Appearing to 'make use' of the hospital (*e.g.* having their child in hospital for permanent care although possessing a large home and having the appearance of being wealthy).

(6) Giving their child too much to eat when they visited.

(7) 'Spoiling' the child when he was at home (*e.g.* feeding him by bottle for many years, so that (according to ward staff) he had been made into a chronically difficult feeder).

It is understandable that staff caring for large numbers of severely handicapped children under what sometimes are very difficult conditions should judge parents in this way. Thus, the unpopularity of parents who have bottle-fed their children for three or four years and have perhaps caused the child to have chronic feeding problems, reflects the pressure felt in under-staffed wards where there might be 30 children to feed and only three staff to do it. The tension caused by a child who has swallowing difficulties and takes more than his share of staff attention at meal-times results in resentment against his parents for 'spoiling him and giving him bad habits'. However, it may have been that local health services failed to give early advice to those parents about the correct methods of feeding a badly handicapped baby.

Parents are sometimes unpopular because they visit *too much* (*i.e.* three or four times a week) and seem to be always in the ward. This applies particularly to older parents, whose handicapped child might be their only child and who had remained at home with them, the centre of their life, until he was aged ten years or older. Some staff do not appreciate that for many years the lives of these older parents probably revolved around the care of their child, and that they miss him and want still to be involved in feeding him, putting him to bed and clothing him. Because these anxious parents continue to show concern about these matters, staff feel that they are being 'checked up' on and that the parents do not trust them with the child. This situation requires counselling on both sides, so that ward staff and parents may understand and accept each other's rôle with the child.

Parents who are ill, or who have some other problems such as bad housing, threatened eviction, debts, another handicapped child at home, or father in prison, are usually regarded sympathetically, especially if they try to continue visiting their child despite the problems. For example, 15-year-old Eden had been in hospital for 12 years. His family was very large and poor, but they always visited Eden every eight weeks, and sometimes took him home for a day. The staff said: "We know his family loves him and do their best for him and give him a nice time. And they're grateful for what we do for him".

That staff often say they like parents to be 'grateful' may be misinterpreted as their wanting parents to feel under an obligation, but in general it is an illustration of the uncertain relationships which exist between staff and parents. They are often confused about their rôles towards each other and the children, because, although the child still belongs to his parents, the institution has taken over the major part of his care. Often this leads to an awkward shyness between staff and parents, which may only be relieved if the staff make real efforts to make parents feel at home in the ward. This may be done quite simply by giving the parents some small task to do for their child, which they may have wanted to do but were reluctant to suggest. For example, four-year-old Olive was taken home for a day and it was bedtime when her mother brought her back. The newest nursing assistant was busy with the child who slept in the cot next to Olive, and she immediately asked Olive's mother: "Do you want to do your little girl? You can share my trolley. Here's fresh nappies, talc and everything. We'll do the kids together". Olive's mother and the young nurse were soon busy together, sharing the trolley and talking as they each put a child to bed. In this way Olive's mother was completely absorbed into the ward scene instead of standing about feeling awkward and having her child taken over by strangers. It was noticeable that that particular nurse's spontaneous way of approaching people was always helpful to parents.

Misunderstandings are sometimes caused because ward staff give an impression of being unfriendly, whereas in reality thay may be trying to hide their own emotions. For example, Nurse Knight said: "When I see Laura's parents I always want to cry. I can hardly bear to look at them, and I just have to turn away. I always think if *only* Laura could walk out of the ward with her brothers and sisters and enjoy life like any other teenager". The basic reasons why parents and staff have difficulties in relating to each other are shyness, misconceptions about each others' rôles, fear of each others' criticisms, the terrible gravity of the children's handicaps, and the lack of knowledge on both sides about how adequately to help the children. These difficulties can be overcome if definite steps are taken by senior staff to give a lead in developing a policy of welcoming parents (see recommendations, pages 16-18). It is most important that parents should feel that they still have something to offer their child and a part to play in his life, even if they cannot visit very often.

Grandparents

Many of the children were visited by their grandparents, as well as by parents, but for eight of the 223 children grandparents were their main family contact. None of these eight children could talk to their grandparents: they all needed feeding, all were incontinent and none could walk. The nurses had great admiration for these grandparents who showed such love and loyalty to their handicapped grandchildren.

Nineteen-year-old Roy had been in hospital for 16 years. His mother had died at his birth, and he had been brain-damaged. His maternal grandfather had visited him every Sunday for 16 years. He always brought a tin of fruit and fed Roy from the tin, with a large spoon which the nurses left out ready for him. The nurses recognised that this regular ceremony meant a great deal to Roy's grandfather.

Six-year-old Lane had been in hospital since the road accident which killed his mother and irreversibly injured his own brain. He had been less than a year old when this accident had occurred. Every Saturday and Sunday his maternal grandparents visited him, gave him his supper and sat cuddling him. His father did not visit so frequently.

Sixteen-year-old Marion has been in a series of long-stay mental handicap hospitals since babyhood. Her parents had emigrated to New Zealand, but her elderly widowed grandmother had always kept close contact with her. Grandmother was now too frail to visit, but the nurses were making efforts to keep her in touch with Marion; for example, one of the nurses had several times taken Marion to visit the grandmother at home for an afternoon.

Parents' associations

Three of the eight hospitals had Parents' Associations. Two of these were Pine and Willows Hospitals (see p. 10). In both these new hospitals the parents, by belonging to the Parents' Associations, could attend meetings to discuss their children and the general organisation of the ward insofar as it affected their children. Discussions included such subjects as getting the right sort of boots for their children, clothing, calipers, wheelchair provision, outings and physiotherapy. Parents were introduced to new staff, and were kept informed of any changes in hospital policy. Some parents helped to paint and furnish the wards. Other activities included coffee mornings, fund-raising and lecture meetings.

The third hospital with a Parents' Association was the old, large, remotely-situated Bay Hospital (described on p. 8). This Association had started in 1974. Not all the wards for severely handicapped children in Bay Hospital had very active parents' groups, which was thought to be largely due to the difficulty in travelling to the hospital, but those that did seemed to have better relationships between parents and ward staff. There had been some initial opposition from administrators to the formation of parents' groups, but the parents—with the support of the senior nursing staff—finally got the idea approved. The nursing officers saw the parent's groups as a means of breaking down the barriers which existed between parents and ward staff. One nurse commented that before 1974 she had seen mothers standing outside ward front-doors until their children had been dressed for their visits; there had been no thought, at that time, of mothers going into the wards and dressing their own children.

What the families did when they visited

What can families *do* when visiting their children who cannot speak to them or run up to them, who may not be able to hold the toys they bring, and who have to be hand-fed any sweets? In some of the wards the parents talked to other parents who were visiting, and obviously this contact was made easier when wards had an active parents' group which held regular meetings and enabled parents to get to know each other.

Sometimes the parents wheeled their children to the League of Friends'

14

canteen in the hospital grounds and had a cup of tea, or took their child for a picnic in the grounds. In Willows Hospital, the ward staff sometimes welcomed parents by giving them a cup of tea, and a biscuit for their handicapped child. A small but thoughtful act like this, initiated by considerate staff, can help to avoid the situation of lonely parents sitting miserably by their child's wheelchair and not knowing what to do or to say.

When brothers and sisters came with their parents to visit the handicapped child, they sometimes played with him by pushing him up and down in his wheelchair. However, if their handicapped sibling was unresponsive, the visiting brothers and sisters tended to play with the more able children in the ward, *i.e.* those who were able to crawl about and say a few words, or perhaps roll a ball. Some appeared to find the visits to the hospital very boring; they sat in the ward and said very little.

How the children reacted to their families

Many of the children showed little obvious response to their families, but it would be misleading to judge from this that the visits meant little to them. Other children smiled, shouted, laughed or wriggled. Some clung tightly when lifted up, and cried bitterly when put down and when their parents left. 20-year-old Sheila always shouted her own name when she saw her parents arrive, and then sang snatches of songs that she had been taught at home before her admission to hospital. She had been living in hospital since the age of six, and her family visited her very frequently.

One 10-year-old child smiled only when her parents came: she had been in hospital for three years and the staff believed that she was always fretting to be at home.

Some children anticipated their parents coming, before they actually arrived in the ward, if they visited regularly on the same day of the week and at the same time. Every Sunday afternoon, 13-year-old Charles waited by the dayroom door for about an hour before his mother appeared. He was ambulant but blind, and had a very close relationship with his mother, although he had been in the hospital for nine years. On very rare occasions Charles was disappointed in the expected visit, then he moaned and pressed his hands to his face in gestures of despair.

What parents expected from the hospital

Parents expected their children to be treated kindly and to be fed well. Few expected them to be cured of the severe handicaps, but most looked for progress and some hoped that their children would eventually learn to speak or to walk. Justifiably, parents expected their children to have the benefits of special services, such as physiotherapy to prevent deformities, speech therapy to aid communication, and occupational therapy to help them to hold a cup or pull on a sock. It can be depressing for parents to discover that these special services, which one expects a hospital to provide, may not be available for their children.

15

RECOMMENDATIONS

Every mental handicap hospital should have a clearly defined and practical policy for helping the families of long-stay multiply handicapped children. Ward staff should be familiar with the policy and should be clear about their own rôle in relation to parents. The policy should not be some ineffectual philosophy, but should give clear guidelines which can be implemented at ward level. Such guidelines would include the following under four main headings: hospital management; helping families to maintain contact; parents' visits; and helping children who are unvisited.

Hospital management

(1) The hospital should have a Families' Association, which would be involved not only in fund-raising and social activities, but also in influencing hospital management insofar as it affects the children (*e.g.* there should be a parent representative on the hospital's management team).

(2) Parents should be invited to attend ward staff meetings.

(3) Parents should be given full information about any changes in hospital administration which might affect their children, for example the possible closure of the physiotherapy department because of lack of staff, or a reduction in ward staff, difficulties in transporting their children to the hospital school, or the lack of speech therapists.

(4) Parents should be informed of any student or post-graduate research taking place in the hospital which might involve their children (*e.g.* in sociology, psychology, medicine, education), and be given some idea of the aims of the research.

Helping families to maintain contact

(5) A member of staff (not necessarily at senior level) who knows the child should be responsible for writing personal letters to parents to give news of their child. The aim would be to keep the parents informed about details such as any outings the child has been on, his reactions, any new clothes he may have been bought recently, any slight progress he might have made, and his general health. These letters would be non-medical, of the kind that would be written by house-parents for a child in residential care who cannot write for himself.

(6) The parents should be invited to join any hospital outings their child goes on: even if they cannot go, they should be given the choice.

(7) If family problems make it likely that the child is at risk of losing contact with his family, the possibility of taking him for short visits to his family should be considered. Perhaps these visits could be organised by student nurses or volunteers if regular ward staff could not be spared.

16

(8) If families find it difficult to get transport to and from the hospital, a system of voluntary transport could be organised.

Parents' visits
(9) Parents should be made to feel physically and emotionally comfortable when they visit.

(10) They should be given a chair to sit down on, beside their child's wheelchair.

(11) If staff are having a tea-break, they should offer a cup of tea to the parents.

(12) If parents like to be alone with their child when they visit, they should be able to go into a bedroom or some other small room which is not in use.

(13) Any progress made by the child, however meagre, should be mentioned to the parents when they visit. It may only be some small achievement, such as the child's lifting his arm unaided when he was being undressed, but the parents should be told about it because it may help them to feel that their child is not a complete write-off.

(14) New ward staff should always be introduced to parents by name, and it should be explained if they are students, temporary staff or new permanent staff.

(15) Parents should be told the names of other children who are near their own child.

(16) Parents should be introduced to other visiting parents in the ward.

(17) Parents should be given the opportunity to help with dressing, feeding and putting their child to bed. If the child is difficult to feed, parents should not be left to struggle with him on their own so that they feel foolish in the presence of staff who may be more experienced in the techniques of feeding difficult children; they should be helped tactfully. If they wish to help with putting their child to bed, they should be shown where all the materials are (clothes, flannels, soap and suchlike) so that they feel at ease in the ward.

Helping children who are unvisited
(18) There should be some special help available to ensure that outside links are maintained for those children who have little or no family contact. Volunteer visitors could become regular 'hospital foster-parents', not necessarily with the idea of taking the children to live at home with them, but in order to take an active part in the unvisited child's life so as to improve his outside contacts. They might take him on outings and holidays, and they could join the Parents' Association as his 'foster-parents'. At present, children may only be officially fostered through being taken into the care of local authorities, but for children in long-stay hospitals who are not officially in care

and whose parents would not agree to them being so, there should be some half-way scheme whereby they might have an adult assigned to them who would take a long-term personal interest in them if their families cannot do so. These 'hospital foster-parents' would have their expenses paid when they visit the child and if they take him out. Such a scheme would enable the child to make a relationship with somebody outside the hospital, in an attempt to improve his life-style.

(19) Unvisited children who are already officially in care, but who have no foster-parents because they have lived for many years in hospital, should be included in the above scheme.

CHAPTER 3

Special Services for the Multiply Handicapped Children

Bearing in mind that multiply handicapped children in long-stay hospitals are said to be there because they need the specialist services of a hospital, this chapter looks at the special services actually being provided for the 223 multiply handicapped children in this study (Table I).

Physiotherapy

The work of physiotherapists in mental handicap hospitals may cover a wide range of activity, including therapy for the long-stay multiply handicapped adults and children, and for adults who may be elderly and/or suffering from arthritis, the effects of strokes, accidents or general sickness; assessment of in-patients and attendance at case conferences on in-patients; assessment and therapy for out-patients; advice and treatment sessions at local special schools; and advice to families. Some physiotherapists are members of their hospital's management team and the district's Health Care Planning Team; some give lectures to parent groups and voluntary organisations and some are involved in teaching student physiotherapists and student nurses.

Table II shows the physiotherapy services available in the hospitals studied. With only 11 physiotherapists working in the eight hospitals, which between them accommodated a total of 4850 mentally handicapped patients, the service is obviously a very sparse one. Three of the hospitals, which between them accommodated 2020 patients, did not employ any physio-

TABLE I

Numbers of specialist staff in the eight hospitals

Hospital	No. of patients	Physio.	Therapists Speech	Occup.	Psychologists	Medical consultants	Social workers
Ash	420	—	—	—	1	2	1*
Bay	1400	—	—	1	2	3	7*
Birch	240	5	1	5	1	2	3*
Elm	1500	1	—	—	1	2	1*
Larch	600	1	—	1	2	3	2*
Oak	200	—	—	—	3	1	†
Willows	200	2½	½	2	3	1	†
Pine	290	1½	1	1½	2	3	†
Totals	4850	11	2½	10½	15	17	14*

*Working from social work department based in the hospitals.
†Called in as required from local authority social services departments.

therapists at all. The services were also unevenly distributed. Five of the 11 therapists were concentrated in one of the smaller hospitals (240 patients), whereas the two biggest hospitals, with 1500 and 1400 patients, had one physiotherapist and none respectively.

The 75 children who were receiving physiotherapy had at least one session a week, and in some cases every day. The reasons why only 75 of the 223 physically disabled children received physiotherapy were:
(A) because no physiotherapists were employed in the hospital;
(B) because the physiotherapists tended to concentrate on the less severely disabled and more responsive children in the wards, and on out-patients, because they considered that a large proportion of the long-term special-care ward children were now beyond effective help from physiotherapists since their limbs were too badly contracted and they made little response to therapy;
(C) because the physiotherapists basically did not believe that severely handicapped children were worth spending professional time on.

Ms. Devitt was in category (C). She had decided to stop giving therapy to the 27 multiply handicapped children in her hospital because she did not think that such severely handicapped children were worth helping. She described the special-care children as "vegetables", and as she was the only physio-

TABLE II

Numbers of children receiving physiotherapy

Hospital		No. multiply handicapped children	No. children receiving physiotherapy	No. physio-therapists employed in hospital	Where therapy given
Ash		24	11*	—	Remedial room
Bay:					
Ward 2	26				
Other wards	7	41	—	—	
	8				
Birch		29	19	5	Ward, and schoolroom adjoining ward
Elm		16	11	1	Remedial room
Larch		27	—	1	
Oak:					
Ward 7	21	28	—	—	
Other ward	7				
Willows		21	11	2½	Ward, and playroom adjoining ward
Pine:					
Ward 8	11				
Ward 10	18	37	23	1½	Physiotherapy department
Other ward	8				
Totals		223	75	11	

*No therapists were employed in the hospital, but the nurses gave therapy, supervised by a physiotherapist from the local Infirmary.

therapist employed in her hospital, her decision meant that the multiply handicapped children were left totally without therapy — despite the fact that a new physiotherapy department costing £72,000 had recently been built in the hospital. Ms. Devitt worked only with small groups of selected, responsive adults, doing movement, dance and yoga sessions.

The physiotherapists in category (B) said that they had conflicting feelings about the morality of *selecting* children to work with (*e.g.* giving priority to out-patients) but they felt that this difficult decision was forced on them by the shortage of therapy staff in the National Health Service, so they had to concentrate on children for whom some progress might be achieved. The choice for some of these physiotherapists was also influenced by job satisfaction, in that they found the young out-patients, especially the babies and under-fives, far more rewarding to work with than the chronically deformed long-stay ward children. Several physiotherapists said they would leave the National Health Service altogether if they had to work entirely with the long-stay multiply handicapped children: "It's the out-patients who keep us alive", one said. In Birch Hospital, which employed five physiotherapists, 60 per cent of the time was given to young out-patients. Another reason for preferring out-patient work was that it brought the therapists professionally satisfying contact with young parents who were eager to receive advice about how to help their disabled babies.

Some physiotherapists felt discouraged at working in special-care wards because they believed that nurses were not in sympathy with their aims. For example, a physiotherapist could spend half an hour placing a child in a good physical position and teaching him to crawl, but when he went back to the ward he might immediately be placed in a very poor position in a bean-bag, or in an ill-fitting chair with his feet dangling awkwardly down.

The difficulties that many nurses appeared to have in appreciating that physiotherapy was not an isolated treatment but had to be a 24-hour way of life for the children if it was going to help them, alternately depressed and irritated the physiotherapy staff and was a major cause of them turning to out-patients for their job satisfaction.

Conflict between nurses and physiotherapists was exacerbated by a number of factors. One was the shortage of nurses to maintain the positions and encourage the movements which the physiotherapists recommended for the children (but therapists were often guilty of not fully appreciating the difficulties of under-staffed wards). Another was the unnecessary bitterness of some nurses, who thought that physiotherapists had an easy job because they did not work with large numbers of children at a time, and did not have to feed, change or toilet the children. Some nurses also had suspicions about the professional skills of physiotherapists, and many had very low expectations for the children and did not have much faith in what the therapists could do for them.

The place where the physiotherapists worked could cause, or prevent, these conflicts. Few things seemed to antagonise nurses more than for their

21

children to be taken away to a separate department and then to be returned later with a cryptic message from someone they did not know, telling them what they must do with the children. On the other hand, when the physiotherapists worked in the wards, the cynicism that some ward staff felt about the effectiveness of physiotherapy was lessened by their being able to see what was being achieved with the children. The nurses also were able to get to know the physiotherapists personally and take part in what the children were doing, and to learn about the aims of therapy.

In two of the five hospitals which had physiotherapists, the therapists worked on the wards and knew the nurses well; sometimes they helped to feed the children at lunch or tea-time. In these two hospitals there was a happier relationship between physiotherapists and nurses, compared with the three hospitals in which the therapists worked in a department away from the ward.

The consultants and senior nurses of Ash Hospital were so concerned at the lack of physiotherapy for their multiply handicapped children that they opened a small 'remedial department'. It was equipped with apparatus and a small pool, and staffed by a State Enrolled Nurse and a Nursing Assistant. They were supervised by the senior physiotherapists of the local Infirmary, who visited them once a week and advised on the work they were doing. They worked with 11 children and concentrated on helping them to sit up, to kneel, crawl and play, and to hold spoons and cups. Although officially they were employed as nurses, these two women were known as 'physio aides', and they worked five days a week from 9.30 until 4.30. The children appeared to be happy in the remedial department, and these two nurses said that they had found tremendous satisfaction in changing from ward work to remedial work. This remedial department was a good solution to the lack of physiotherapy in Ash Hospital, but the scheme seemed likely to fail because of the antagonism of some ward nurses. The physio aides were described as "just jumped-up nurses" and there was some opposition to their suggestions about how the children should be sat and fed.

Lack of a physiotherapy service for long-stay children can cause gross deformities of the children's limbs and spines, which give them considerable discomfort and make them difficult to dress, feed and wash. The multiply handicapped children in Bay Hospital were pitiful examples of what can happen when children live for years in a hospital in which there is a permanent shortage of specialist staff. Some of the children had developed scissored legs to the degree that it was almost impossible to get a pair of pants on them. 15-year-old Margaret, who had lived in Bay Hospital for 13 years, was fixed permanently into a sideways twisted position, with her legs drawn up in a fetal position. It was impossible to place her in a chair: she had to lie on her side all the time, and because one side of her face was permanently pressed downwards she could only see out of one eye. When she was fed, the food tended to trickle out of the lower corner of her mouth as fast as it was put into the upper corner.

Bay Hospital had a large, well-equipped physiotherapy department, but it was not used. Over the previous 12 years a total of five therapists had been employed there, but none had remained for long: for the last year the hospital had not been able to attract any physiotherapist. It was understandable that it was difficult to get a physiotherapist to work for long in Bay Hospital because it accommodated 1400 long-stay patients and was situated in the countryside. Any new therapist was likely to become quickly demoralised by a feeling of professional isolation when faced with the problems of having to develop, virtually single-handed, a therapy service in such a large and remote institution. 17 miles away from Bay Hospital there was a small voluntary school for 132 cerebral-palsied children. It employed five full-time physiotherapists, two physio aides, four full-time speech therapists, and one full-time occupational therapist. These therapists found immense professional satisfaction in working in the small, modern school close to the city, and they were stimulated by the professional support they received from each other. When they were asked what they knew about Bay Hospital, one of the school therapists answered: "we find the whole idea of it is very depressing. We would find it so lonely to work in a place like that".

It would seem that large institutions in remote country districts are not the best places in which to put multiply handicapped children who require the help of physiotherapists.

It was significant that Birch and Willows Hospitals, the two hospitals employing the most physiotherapists (five and 2½ respectively), had the following in common:
(1) both were small (Birch 240 patients, Willows 200 patients);
(2) they were not isolated — Birch was within easy reach of a University town and Willows was in a small market town;
(3) the physiotherapists were members of an interested and enthusiastic inter-disciplinary team of other professionals, and they did not feel professionally isolated.

Speech therapy

Two of the eight hospitals had one full-time speech therapist each, and a third hospital had one part-time speech therapist. They did not work with any of the 223 multiply handicapped children in the study. They assessed out-patients, advised families and local special schools, and worked with small groups of able, adult patients. As with physiotherapists, the shortage of speech therapists encouraged the selection of patients: those children who were least likely to show obvious progress (the long-stay severely handicapped children) would be least likely to be selected for therapy.

Larch Hospital had once had a connection with a teaching hospital's speech therapy department, and the special-care ward staff had been advised about feeding and speech development; student speech therapists had also worked in the ward as part of their training. The principal speech therapist gave two reasons for discontinuing this arrangement:
(1) "It was a waste of time trying to get a correct feeding programme going in the ward, when the nurses would not follow it." (Conflicts between nurses and

speech therapists can be bitter, because speech therapists are essentially involved in advising on feeding methods, and nurses understandably see feeding as their particular domain and resent any interference. Arguments about how the children should be fed are sometimes so difficult to resolve that the speech therapists eventually cease to give advice. 134 of the 223 children had chronic feeding problems and were fed on mashed food. Consistent advice from speech therapists may have helped them to chew solids and swallow correctly.)

(2) "It became a matter of choosing priorities, and mental handicap is low on our list of priorities. If we have to make a choice between treating a businessman so that he can get back to work after a stroke, or going to the mental handicap hospital to help children who will never work, then it is plain where our priorities must lie." (The decisions that professionals take when faced with the moral dilemma of having to choose priorities are increasingly rationalised by reference to how much work output the chosen patient will be able to plough back into the nation's economy!)

Communication

Many multiply handicapped children have such grave physical disabilities, combined with severe mental retardation, that they cannot achieve normal language. Their problems of movement and hand deformities may also be thought to prevent them from communicating by recognisable hand signs. However, many of the children in this study were able to vocalise, smile appropriately, make eye-contact, 'point' with their eyes, and wave. Some nurses had got children to say "mmmm" as they were being bathed, or had acquired good eye-contact with them, and others had encouraged children to indicate by facial expressions what they wanted to eat and drink. These primary communication abilities might have been developed in some organised and constructive manner if speech therapists, nurses and teachers had worked together and drawn up a plan of how each child could be helped to communicate according to his particular ability, but none of the hospitals had such plans.

When staff have no system of communicating with the children, it is possible that some children's attempts to attract attention and make social responses may deteriorate into apparently meaningless, and often irritating, cries and movements. It is not enough for one or two of the staff to have their particular children who they can 'get through to' in their own way; instead, there needs to be a concerted, organised effort made by all staff to use a common technique of communication.

It is essential that staff carefully assess how each child might be helped to communicate; that they share this information and inform all new members of staff what has so far been achieved; that they perhaps introduce the children to the widely accepted common gestures used by deaf people (British Sign Language); and that they ensure the signs are used generally throughout the child's daily life, and not merely on an occasional sessional basis.

Knowledge about how to communicate with multiply handicapped children is still very much in its infancy. Indeed, the earliest published report on the use of signing with mentally handicapped people appeared as recently as 1969[5]. This referred to work done in an American State hospital with mentally handicapped students aged between seven and 41 years. Dr. Chris Kiernan, of the Thomas Coram Research Unit, University of London Institute of Education, has not only made extensive reviews of all the published literature on communication systems, but he is also directing a research project into how to teach communication systems to multiply handicapped children and how staff can best use such systems. In a paper written for the *British Journal of Mental Subnormality*[6], Dr. Kiernan discusses all the present systems of communication — Makaton, Paget-Gorman Sign System, British Sign Language, Bliss, Premack, and others. Anybody wishing to be up-to-date in this field should read this important paper.

It is possible that many children in special-care wards are being under-estimated, and incorrectly judged to be incapable of communicating, solely because the hospital staff are uninformed about techniques of communication. Perhaps the following story concerning a child I worked with prior to making this present study may be a helpful example of how a non-speaking multiply handicapped child may be helped to communicate:

In the early 1970s, when I was working as a teacher in a long-stay children's hospital, a cerebral-palsied, hearing, non-ambulant child of six years old, who had been assessed as severely mentally subnormal and who had no physical ability in his hands and very little head-control, learnt to use a 'word board' which was gradually built up for him on a system of only using words which had some important personal meaning for him. Beginning with one written word, his own name, he progressed to read the names of other children, names and addresses of people who were significant to him, favourite colours and food, holiday place-names, special dates (Christmas, birthdays, Easter) and words such as cross, sad and happy, which were descriptive of easily mimed emotions. The learning of some words (*e.g.* car, tree, house) was assisted by pictures. As he had no speech, this method of communication naturally required a one-to-one concentration, but it was often possible to create a positive learning situation for him and other children by grouping children around his board so all shared in the attention. In the initial stages of his learning, he used his hand to wave towards the words or letters, or he eye-pointed, or indicated by facial expression 'yes' or 'no' to someone else's pointing and questions. At first, the work demanded a great deal of repetitive questions, but within three years he learnt to read simple infant-school reading books, and finally to spell out

5. Sutherland, G. F., Beckett, J. W. (1969) 'Teaching the mentally retarded sign language.' *Journal of Rehabilitation of the Deaf,* 2 (4), 56-60.
6. Kiernan, C. (1977) 'Alternatives to speech: a review of research on manual and other alternative forms of communication with the mentally handicapped and other non-communicating populations.' *British Journal of Mental Subnormality,* 23, 6-28.

words from an alphabet board. He is now able to use a 'Possum' typewriter. He had two word-boards, one in his schoolroom and one in his ward. They were easily made, being simply a large sheet of paper on which the words were very clearly written in squares, and the paper was slotted under a large sheet of clear perspex, which had been fastened securely onto his ward and school table-tops by the hospital carpenter. He could still see the words as he ate his meals on the table, or played in school, rolled pastry or finger-painted. The perspex could be easily washed, without harming the paper underneath, and the paper was easily changed as new words were added.

Occupational therapists

Although there were the equivalent of 10½ qualified occupational therapists working in the eight hospitals, only one had offered to advise the special-care ward staff about their children (and this offer had not been taken advantage of in a very active manner). Another recently appointed occupational therapist said that she would like to work with children but she was unable to do so because the terms of her appointment required her to work only with the adults in the hospital.

Occupational therapists in mental handicap hospitals are rarely involved with the long-stay children. At one time their work was to occupy, assess and train adult in-patients, and to develop industrial and craft-work departments. Now, in addition to still being involved in this traditional work with adults, some occupational therapists are assessing child out-patients and giving advice in the community. However, in spite of their expanding work, they do not yet have an active rôle in the children's special-care wards.

Occupational therapy complements education and ward care, so there is a need for the therapists to take more part in the care of long-stay multiply handicapped children. There are many areas in which their professional advice would be valuable to nurses and teachers, especially in how to develop the children's hand abilities: they could advise on how to teach a child to hold a cup, or push a ball, pick up a toy, pull off his own socks or help to wriggle his arms from his cardigan when he is being undressed, or to hold a flannel at washing time. Meagre as these achievements may seem, the learning of them could reduce the total helplessness of the children and prevent the hand deformities caused by not using the hands.

Sixty-six of the 223 children in the study were unable to grasp objects because their hands were so affected by their handicaps and allied deformities. The other 157 children had some grasp ability, but only 11 of these could dress or wash themselves, and only 53 could feed themselves. One wonders if these figures of achievement might have been higher if the 157 children with some grasp ability had received the professional skills of an occupational therapist.

Psychologists

There were 15 full-time psychologists in the eight hospitals. Their work covered both the traditional forms of mental handicap hospital psychology (testing the patients' intellectual abilities, keeping records of tests, and giving recommendations about future discharge) and the more modern forms (developing behaviour modification programmes to help children and adults with behaviour problems, advising in local special schools, attending clinics, assessing out-patients, and devising programmes of child-management for parents to follow at home if their child needed systematic help in learning how to feed himself or in how to use the lavatory). Some of the psychology departments were also involved with training students, and with post-graduate research.

The 15 psychologists had very little contact with the special-care wards, apart from Oak Hospital (see p. 137), where it was claimed that a number of children had been taught to feed themselves through the principles of behaviour modification. The psychologist in one hospital said he "could only spare time to work with those mentally handicapped people who can earn a place in the community", and "why waste time and resources on teaching spastic children to grasp bricks when they'll never go out into the community?"

It would appear that, although the majority of the psychologists in this study had developed a new professional image and were extending their work into the community and becoming highly skilled in helping mentally handicapped people who had behaviour problems, they had not yet developed any constructive rôle with long-stay multiply handicapped children.

The effect of the ward environment on the development of multiply handicapped children was not the subject of serious study by the psychologists, only one of whom was attempting to evolve a new rôle in respect of long-stay patients and the organisation of their day. She thought that psychologists could help in developing well-organised ward activities, based on the *Bezigheidstherapie* (activation therapy) which occurs in mental handicap institutions in The Netherlands.

Student psychologists

Although the special-care wards rarely saw the psychologists, a student psychologist was sometimes assigned to the ward to work with one particular child. This would usually be a child who had a problem, such as head-banging, hand-chewing or regurgitating his food. The student would devise a programme for the child and keep records of his responses, and would concentrate on him for a period of perhaps six weeks. With one-to-one contact over this period of time the child invariably showed changes in his behaviour, but usually regressed after the student had left. A few months later another psychology student was likely to arrive and start another period of concentrated work with the same child, devising another programme and keeping more records. When this happened the nurses, understandably, were annoyed because they thought the child was being 'exploited' by the students. They saw little long-term benefit for the individual children who had to participate in the work of these transient psychology students, and they wondered how fair it was to the children. The nurses themselves were unable to maintain the programmes efficiently because shortages of nursing staff made it difficult to organise the ward so as to allow any one child to have regular and sustained attention from one particular member of the staff.

Medical consultants

Mental handicap hospital consultants are at present in an anomalous position because the traditional position of Medical Superintendent has been abolished and the hospitals are now managed by a multi-disciplinary team. This often means an overt shuffling of power between the medical consultant, the senior nursing officer, the principal psychologist, and the hospital administrator. So, to develop a position in the community as professional advisers on all matters concerned with mental handicap would seem a useful way for consultants in mental handicap hospitals to retain their professional power.

The majority of the 17 consultants in the eight hospitals were developing this community adviser rôle, and their out-patient lists and extramural professional activities were increasing.

Several consultants admitted that their hospitals were providing accommodation for children who did not need constant medical care. One said: "at the same time, it must be realised that local authorities cannot be forced to implement community care, so there is no choice for doctors except to admit the children to hospitals, especially if the families have got problems". Although he was based in a mental handicap hospital, this consultant was active in supporting families within the community; he advised them on their children's development, attended paediatric clinics and committees connected with mental handicap, advised at local special schools, and did all he could to influence the development of good community care locally.

The consultant in Willows Hospital, in addition to developing her community work, also took over-all responsibility for the 200 in-patients of the hospital for any special help they needed from other consultants (orthopaedic surgeons, ophthalmic surgeons, neurologists, dental surgeons). She acted as a medical spokesman for the in-patients, with the purpose of persuading other medical specialists that a comprehensive health-care service must be as readily available to people living in mental handicap hospitals as it is for non-handicapped people in the community, and must be of a similar standard.

However, that consultant's approach did not seem to be so easy for all the mental handicap consultants. Some appeared to be daunted by their colleagues in other fields, especially by those in orthopaedic surgery. An example of this was seen in Elm Hospital, where 13-year-old Rachel had been living for six years. She could use her hands, but because of grave hip-deformities caused by hip dislocations, she was unable to sit up. She had to spend all her life on her back, propped with pillows, and her view of the world was very restricted. Also, because her legs were at right angles to her body, she suffered from pressure sores on the outside edges of her knees. Rachel could communicate by facial expressions and with a few words, she showed an ability to choose her own food, and appeared to have certain favourite nurses. The mental handicap consultant referred Rachel to the orthopaedic surgeon at the local hospital for advice about giving her corrective surgery to enable her to sit up, but the surgeon declined to operate because she was "in such poor condition" (letter from the orthopaedic surgeon to the mental handicap hospital consultant). The consultant in the mental handicap hospital said that the orthopaedic surgeon's decision probably had been prompted by the fact that Rachel was mentally handicapped and living permanently in a mental handicap hospital, and although he recognised that the surgeon's discrimination was unfair, he did not like to challenge him on the issue because "it is difficult for a psychiatrist to query the decisions of an orthopaedic surgeon and it would cause bad feeling".

It would seem, therefore, that multiply handicapped children who live permanently in mental handicap hospitals may be discriminated against by other specialists unless the mental handicap consultants are prepared to act as professional spokesmen for them. It is possible that Rachel would have received her orthopaedic treatment if she had been living in Willows Hospital, where the consultant was more outspoken in her dealings with other medical specialists.

In many cases the mental handicap consultants too easily accepted that multiply handicapped children were beyond help. For example, they did not seek treatment for the children's bad and mis-shapen teeth, or for facial deformities which might have been corrected by surgery. By not insisting that specialist services should be available for multiply handicapped children, these consultants condoned the idea that multiply handicapped children were less worthy of treatment than ordinary children, and in doing so they lessened the children's chances of social acceptance because it is not easy for society to accept children with gross physical defects.

Although the majority of the 17 consultants were busy developing an active professional position in the community, some were so overwhelmed by the many problems in their institutions that they had retreated into their offices and were rarely seen, either in the community or in their hospital. They had little influence on the way of life of the in-patients. One newly-appointed consultant was given special responsibility for the children, but five months after his appointment he had not familiarised himself with the needs of the children in the special-care ward: the Ward Sister said: "he never comes near". A careful medical assessment of the children in that ward would have revealed that they had many health problems which needed to be dealt with by a consultant acting as spokesman and co-ordinator of medical services for them: there were a number who might have benefited from referral to ophthal-mologists, audiologists and orthopaedic surgeons, and there was also a need to establish why none of the children were receiving the speech therapy and physiotherapy services they needed.

In five of the eight hospitals, some of the children were suffering from what can only be described as the poverty conditions of the 19th century, i.e.

chronic catarrh, runny ears, sore eyes, skin diseases, chronic recurring stomach upsets, bad teeth and worms. Some of these disorders might be ascribed to the fact that large numbers of children were living together in somewhat unhygienic conditions (*e.g.* sharing washing water, flannels and towels), but they might have been avoided if the consultants had given a stronger lead in supervising the general health care of the children, and if the nursing administration had kept more in touch with what was happening at ward level.

In some of the hospitals, general practitioners came in twice a week to oversee the general health of the children. They diagnosed any childhood complaints, prescribed necessary medicines and treated minor accidents, but they did not feel that they were in a position to make positive criticisms about the general standard of health care for long-stay children.

Social workers

After the reorganisation of the National Health Service in 1974, social workers in hospitals became employed by the local authority instead of by hospital authorities. However, hospitals with long-established social work departments have retained them, and five of the eight hospitals in the study had their own social work departments, employing a total of 14 qualified social workers. In the other three hospitals the social workers came as required from the social service departments of the local authority, and they attended occasional case conferences and out-patient clinics at the hospitals. The hospital-based social workers saw themselves as members of a professional team, attempting to give a service to mentally handicapped people and their families. Their work was predominently community-oriented. They attended out-patient clinics, visited families, supervised the discharge and after-care of adult patients, advised on the family's housing, social service benefits, the Disabled Persons Act, the Family Fund, and employment. They also liaised between the hospital and the family when a child required short-term care.

None of the social workers in the study took any interest in the life style of the children in the special-care wards; the only contact they had with the wards was when it was necessary to arrange an occasional period of short-term care for a multiply handicapped child whose parents needed a break from his care. Indeed, only one of the 14 social workers in the study said that she believed social workers ought to take some responsibility for trying to improve the environment for long-stay patients. The other 13 did not think so: one said that social workers were "in no position to criticise the standard of child-care in the wards"; another that she "did not have anything to do with the special-care wards, as those children will never be discharged".

This total lack of involvement with the life style of long-stay hospital children is a common failing of social workers throughout the country, and does not only apply to those met in this study. Social workers, as a profession, have always been reluctant to make a stand about the need to improve the daily care of long-stay hospital children. This may be illustrated by the way in which

30

they fulfil their official supervisory duties of those children who are in the care of local authorities but who are living in long-stay hospitals. For example, when doing a review on an 'in-care' child, a social worker will go to the ward and look at the child's case-notes to assure himself that 'all is well' with the child, but he will not make recommendations for improving the child's care; for example his need for mothering, continuity of staff, more play, outings, personal possessions and holidays. An example of this was seen in Birch Hospital, where 11-year-old Daphne, a cerebral-palsied child who had been taken into care, had been living for four years. The senior social worker said that she was shortly going to do Daphne's review (as required every six months), and she described this review as requiring her to visit Daphne's ward to "see that she is still all right". She said that she did not believe it was her responsibility to ask questions about Daphne's care "in case it upset the hospital staff". However, if that social worker had been visiting Daphne in a foster home or a children's Home in the community, she would have closely examined the environment to see if it was conducive to Daphne's healthy emotional and physical development, and she would have made a report to the social services department if the substitute home seemed unsuitable.

Observations made in Daphne's ward showed that she led the typical deprived life of any multiply handicapped child living in a kindly but under-staffed and over-crowded ward. For example, during a period of 10 hours and 20 minutes, Daphne received only 67 minutes attention, and that attention was concerned only with her physical needs.

Social workers seem not to recognise the deprivation suffered by children in long-stay hospitals, and their failure to expect the same standards of child care in hospitals as they would expect for a child in residential care in the community serves to perpetuate the deprivation.

The reasons why social workers do not take action about the conditions in the wards may be twofold. They may not consider that gravely multiply handicapped children merit the same standards of child care that would be demanded for ordinary children living in community-based substitute homes. Also, they are wary of the hospital hierarchy and are reluctant to criticise in case they upset the doctors or the nurses. (A Director of Social Services said that when he had been a child-care officer and visited hospitals to see children who were in the care of his local authority social service department, he had thought the ward conditions were "very dreadful" but never said anything in case the staff were upset.)

Whatever the reason, the result has been that social workers have turned a blind eye to the deprivation suffered by long-stay hospital children, although it might be expected that they, more than any other professionals, would have been able to influence standards of child care in long-stay hospitals, especially in the years since the Curtis Report[7] and the subsequent appointment between 1948 and 1968 of child-care officers with a special responsibility for

7. Curtis Report (1946) *Report of the Committee on the Care of Children.* (Chairman: Dame Myra Curtis.) London: H.M.S.O.

children in substitute homes, and since knowledge has increased about the effects of institutional care on child development (Bowlby 1951, Tizard 1964: see Recommended Further Reading, p. 159).

Wheelchairs, furniture and aids

Wheelchairs

Only three of the eight hospitals had sufficient wheelchairs and small pushchairs for the children in their special-care wards. The other five hospitals had old and broken chairs. Confusion about who actually had administrative responsibility for repair and ordering of wheelchairs meant that some children remained without a chair: for example, 11-year-old Hugh's wheelchair was sent away to be repaired, but nine months later it had still not been returned and nobody knew what had become of it. Hugh had a very large head and his wheelchair had to be specially weighted to prevent him tipping over. Without the chair he could not go to hospital-school, nor be taken for a walk around the grounds; he had to lie on the floor of the ward all the time. The nurses were worried that after nine months of lying on the floor Hugh's neck muscles would have lost the ability to support the weight of his head.

In Elm Hospital there were only three very old, broken wheelchairs for 16 cerebral-palsied children. Outside the ward there was a rusting pile of broken wheelchairs but nobody knew who was responsible for removing them, and it was said that no new wheelchairs could be issued until the old ones were returned to the region's wheelchair centre. This shortage of wheelchairs meant that the children could not be taken out for walks on sunny days.

One ward sister, worried about the lack of a repair service for wheelchairs, used to take chairs home with her if they needed minor repairs, and her father mended them.

In several of the hospitals the children were put in unsuitable wheelchairs: for example, in Oak Hospital, 12-year-old Percy usually sat for eight hours a day in a chair without a foot-rest, and his feet, which were generally bare, dangled uncomfortably down over a narrow iron bar.

Many of the Hospital Advisory Service reports on long-stay hospitals have referred to the poor facilities for maintaining wheelchairs, and occasional circulars are issued by the DHSS regarding wheelchair arrangements. However, it appears that these circulars are largely ignored: in April 1975, Circular HSC(IS)137 stated: 'At some long-stay hospitals, particularly those for the mentally handicapped, it appears that no formal arrangements exist for reviewing the continuing suitability of wheelchairs used by permanently disabled children. In such circumstances, it is strongly recommended that arrangements be made with the Manager of the nearest Artificial Limb and Appliance Centre for the wheelchair requirements of these children to be reviewed at regular intervals.' The title of this circular was *Wheelchair Users in Long-stay Hospitals*, and it was sent to all Regional Health Authorities, Area Health Authorities, and Boards of Governors, marked 'For Action'.

Furniture

There was a general lack of suitable furniture for physically handicapped children. Only two of the eight hospitals had small tables and chairs at which the children could be seated for meals. It was common for children to be fed on the floor or lying in bean-bags, the nurses crouching in front of them; or they were lifted onto high kitchen-type chairs, where they remained with their feet dangling unsupported (a very poor position for cerebral-palsied children to be in). Again, the lack of table surfaces of the correct height for the children to have their plates on meant that they could not attempt to feed themselves; they had to be fed by staff, and this encouraged their total dependence and even made it difficult for them to see what was on their plates.

Furniture and equipment was often ordered by administrators who did not understand the particular needs of handicapped children, and who did not ask the advice of nurses and therapists: the likely result was a proliferation of attractive but unhelpful furniture in the wards. For example, smart little armchairs had been ordered, but they tended to make the children flop back into an awkward position which they could not change. Many of the 223 children spent nine or ten hours a day in such chairs. The armchairs did not have trays fitted to them, on which toys could have been placed, and having nothing with which to occupy their hands, it was not surprising that a number of the children developed habits of sucking their hands and chewing their clothes.

Bean-bags have now become fashionable in wards because their brilliant colours brighten the environment, but there is a tendency to use them indiscriminately in special-care wards. They have a purpose in providing a child with a change of position for a short while, and they can be used to prop up a child so that he may see more clearly what is going on in the ward. But bean-bags are not a good substitute for a chair designed by physiotherapists to comfortably fit a child's special needs and aid his independence. Such individually designed chairs can sometimes be made in the hospital's carpentry shop, being cut-down old wooden chairs and fitted with a suitable foot-rest and an adjustable tray for the child's toys and his cup and plate at meal-times. However, this individual approach to furniture was only seen in two of the eight hospitals.

The indiscriminate use of unsuitable armchairs and bean-bags was not only detrimental to the physical position of cerebral-palsied children, but was also socially very isolating because they restricted the children's movements and prevented social interaction. Severely handicapped children need periods on the floor when they can touch, poke, kick and hold other children, and wriggle about and stretch, but many of the 223 children lived all the time in separate bean-bags and armchairs and had no opportunities for social inter-action.

Aids

There was also a general shortage of aids to help children become toilet-trained, for example of 'potty chairs', which may be safely placed over a conventional lavatory to enable unsteady cerebral-palsied children to sit without falling, and of the small box-like chairs with a hole in the seat to take a pot, which may help younger cerebral-palsied children to become potty-trained. Six of the eight hospitals had neither of these aids, which meant that if a child was not steady enough to sit on a lavatory or a pot without support, he never got the chance to become toilet-trained.

The dearth of occupational therapy advice in special-care wards meant that there was also a shortage of small aids, such as specially designed spoons, plates and cups, which might have made feeding or drinking easier for the children. There was even a shortage of non-slip mats, the simple but invaluable aid to keep a child's plate steady while he is being fed or is trying to feed himself.

It might have been a help if the ward staff had been given independence to seek furniture and aids on their own initiative. Several of the hospitals had Spastics Society day-centres and schools within travelling distance, and these centres might have been a positive link with the special-care wards, sharing information about suitable aids and furniture and where to obtain them. However, there was no contact at all between the special-care wards and the centres being run in the community.

Aids for sensory handicaps

Children who were deaf or blind, or both, or who suffered from hearing loss or partial sight, were not receiving the special help that they needed (*e.g.* glasses, hearing-aids, or toys which might have been of special interest to children with sensory handicaps). 33 of the children were known to be blind, and it was said that approximately 50 per cent might have a hearing loss, but the majority had not had their handicaps fully assessed and the staff were so unsure of the extent of the children's sensory handicaps that no accurate figures for partial sight or deafness could be obtained (see p. 2).

There was confusion, too, about how deaf children could be helped to communicate, or how to teach blind children about their environment. Only one of the 223 children was receiving any intensive, specialist educational help with her sensory handicaps (see p. 68). Because of this lack of help, it is possible that some of the children were functioning at a lower level than they might have done, and there was a risk of increase in handicap. For example, if a child with partial sight is not helped to make use of the little sight he does have, then that sight may become virtually useless to him and he will function as a blind child.

It was frequently said by nurses and teachers that severely handicapped children could not wear hearing-aids or glasses, and this point could be appreciated because the grave shortages of nurses meant that the children's movements could not be continuously supervised and their glasses or hearing-aids could soon fall off. There was also the likelihood of the more able children pulling the aids from the other child's head. These problems of how to keep hearing-aids and glasses on mentally handicapped children who live in over-crowded, under-staffed wards are almost insoluble; however, it might have been helpful if the ward staff and school staff had had some instruction about the value and use of these aids (*i.e.* how to turn on a hearing-aid, the right number for it to be set at for a particular child, how to check that it was working properly and how to change the battery, and how to make (or where to order) a small harness to support the child's aid). It might also have been helpful if some means could have been worked out whereby every child had some period of the day during which he wore his glasses and/or his hearing-aid and had some special supervision in keeping it on; and if attempts were made at the same time to encourage him to respond and notes were made of his responses. But of course such a scheme would depend very much on an increase in ward staff.

Ward design

In some wards the actual architectural design was so unsuitable that it decreased the children's chances of making progress and being more independent. The special-care ward in one hospital had been built in the 1930s and re-designed in the 1960s. There were no wash-basins for the children to use and no normal taps. In the bathroom there was a long, shallow trough, divided into four sections; above the trough there was a long pipe with twelve openings. When a key on the wall was turned, a thin spray of water came from the twelve openings and fell into the trough. The trough had no plugs; there were merely four large holes down which the water drained continuously. This had been designed for the purpose of mass-washing the children, but the nurses found the key-system so tedious, and the continuous running away of the water so impracticable, that they never used the trough. Instead, they washed the children from small plastic bowls, laying them on their beds to do so, and they used the trough as a stand to store laundry bags on. The existence of this trough meant that the children in that ward could never have the experience of turning on a tap, dangling their hands in a wash-basin full of water, washing their own hands and faces, pulling up a plug and watching water run away, and learning about how to mix hot and cold water.

Epilepsy

Of the 223 children, 138 had epilepsy. Children's fits are a cause of great anxiety for parents and may be one of the reasons for a child's admittance to a long-stay hospital. It was rather surprising to find that epilepsy was not causing obvious problems in the wards; during the course of this study only two children went into status because of major fits, and both remained in their wards and made a good recovery within 24 hours. Possibly the reason why epilepsy did not seem to cause much anxiety in the wards was that the majority of the children were immobile and tended to be anchored in one place all day, and their medication was given regularly.

The main worry about epilepsy in the special-care wards appeared to be

35

the side-effects caused by the medication the children were on. In some cases this was causing gross deterioration of the children's gums, with subsequent bleeding and excessive dribbling, and other children appeared to be on drugs which were causing them muzziness, poor vision and giddiness. In some of the wards the children were being changed to different drugs, and the nurses exressed some concern that these new drugs appeared to cause the children to lose their balance: for example three children were having difficulty in keeping their balance when crawling, although at one time they had crawled quite steadily. In this case the doctors were in close contact with the nurses about the way in which these three children were reacting to their new drug, but the nurses in other special-care wards felt that doctors did not do sufficient monitoring and re-assessment of medication, and thought it possible that some children were being given neither the most suitable drug nor the correct dosage.

SUMMARY AND RECOMMENDATIONS

Physiotherapy

Eleven physiotherapists were employed in the eight hospitals. Only 75 of the 223 multiply handicapped children were receiving some type of physio-therapy.

(1) Ward staff should be regarded as part of the physiotherapy services. All special-care ward staff should have opportunities to attend the children's therapy sessions, and they should be given a basic knowledge of the principles of physiotherapy.

(2) Therapy sessions preferably should take place in the wards, and ward staff should participate.

(3) Hospitals without a physiotherapist should set up their own 'physio-aide' service, the nurses working as aides, supervised by the area or district physiotherapist.

(4) If a physiotherapist decides to stop treating a child, she should account for her decision to the hospital's multi-disciplinary management team. Any decision to withhold treatment should be written into the child's case-notes and signed by the management team. The area physiotherapist should also be informed, and the child's parents should also be kept informed and should be free to appeal against the decision.

Speech therapy

Two full-time and one part-time speech therapists were employed in the eight hospitals. None of the 223 children received speech therapy.

(1) to (4) above apply here also.

(5) Studies should be undertaken into methods of communicating with

multiply handicapped children, involving all professional disciplines, with the aim of devising forms of communication which could be used easily by all ward staff during the daily routines of caring for the children. These would be based on each child's individual abilities, however meagre.

Occupational therapy

The equivalent of 10½ qualified occupational therapists worked in the eight hospitals, but apart from the one instance of advice being offered by one therapist, none of the 223 children received occupational therapy.

(6) All special-care ward children should be assessed by an occupational therapist, especially with a view to developing the children's hand skills. Ward staff should be encouraged to seek advice from occupational therapists as to how to teach special skills to individual children.

Psychologists

A total of 15 psychologists worked in the eight hospitals. 14 children had been taught to feed themselves on the advice of psychologists. Other children had also been 'taken on' by student psychologists, but this gave only very inconsistent help.

(7) Psychologists might study the effects of the actual ward environment on children's behaviour (*e.g.* no attention = bizarre habits), and use their findings to influence positive changes in the present methods of child care in long-stay wards.

(8) The practice of using particular children repeatedly for psychology students to test programmes on should be discontinued, unless it can be shown to be in the best interests of the children.

Medical consultants

In general, the 17 medical consultants seemed to be uncertain about how to help multiply handicapped children. Only in one hospital did the consultant see it as her rôle to act as spokesman for the children in obtaining specialist medical services, *e.g.* orthopaedic care.

(9) Children living in long-stay special-care wards should receive the same standard of health care as children living in the community.

(10) Consultants in mental handicap hospitals should ensure that other specialists give their services to the children, without discrimination.

(11) Consultants should be accountable to the multi-disciplinary management team for the health care the long-stay children receive.

(12) General practitioners going into special-care wards should make a report to the hospital's management team, to the Family Practitioner Committee, or to the District Management Team if they consider that the environment of the

ward is having an adverse effect on the children's physical and emotional wellbeing.

Social workers
The 14 social workers in the eight hospitals had little interest in the living conditions of the long-stay children.

(13) Social workers should take a leading rôle in establishing better patterns of child care in the wards, and should look at the wards in the same way as they would look at a substitute home in the community; that is, what effect the whole environment might be having on the children's development.

Special aids, equipment and furniture
These were all inadequate, and there was confusion about how to obtain new aids and equipment, or how to repair or replace old aids and equipment.

(14) Ward staff should be familiar with the administration of wheelchair services.

(15) Before they order furniture, administrators should seek advice from nurses and therapists who know the children.

(16) Staff who know the children should be encouraged to visit centres which specialise in equipment for disabled children.

(17) Children with sensory handicaps should be carefully assessed and issued with appropriate glasses and hearing-aids. Staff should be taught how to help children use these aids, and should be fully aware of their importance.

(18) If special advice is needed about the use, care and maintenance of hearing-aids, contact should be made with the local education authority audiology services.

General recommendations
(19) Some one person should act as a *co-ordinator of services* for handicapped children living in long-stay hospitals. This co-ordinator might have trained originally as a nurse, teacher, social worker, doctor, therapist or administrator, or might be a parent of a handicapped child. The co-ordinator's brief would be to ensure that no child is left without the services he needs.

(20) A child should not live in a long-stay hospital unless he needs special services which can only be provided in hospital, and it can be demonstrated that he gets these services.

CHAPTER 4

The Community

The statement that "people outside don't want to know about *these* kids" was made frequently by special-care ward staff. This chapter discusses the contact that the following groups of people had with the children in this study, and their knowledge about the children's problems:

(1) Administrators of local authority residential services for mentally handicapped children.
(2) Teachers in local special schools.
(3) Members of Community Health Councils.
(4) Voluntary organisations.
(5) Individual volunteers in the hospitals.

Administration of local authority residential services for mentally handicapped children

None of the eight local authorities provided community accommodation which might have enabled the discharge of any of the 223 multiply handicapped children. Local authority homes offered permanent places only to children who had some degree of independence, *i.e.* those who were toilet-trained, ambulant and able to feed themselves. If a non-ambulant child could not live at home with his own family, he was admitted to hospital. As mentioned earlier (p. 4), only one local authority had future plans to provide residential accommodation for multiply handicapped children, and these would provide only five places over a five-year period.

Local authority social service administrators who were responsible for residential accommodation were of the opinion that it would be impossible to accommodate multiply handicapped children in the community: for example, the Homes Officer of one local authority said: "we cannot help children in the wheelchair category—they are for hospital". Another said: "incontinent wheelchair children are a problem for the hospitals, not a problem for local authorities to deal with".

Local authority decisions to exclude multiply handicapped children from their plans for residential care are no doubt influenced by the 1971 White Paper[8], which clearly implied that people with multiple handicaps needed to be accommodated in hospital. For example, it stated:

"If and when a mentally handicapped child or adult has to leave his family home, a suitable substitute home must be provided. Some will need to go to

8. Department of Health and Social Security (1971) *Better Services for the Mentally Handicapped*. Cmnd. 4683. London: H.M.S.O.

hospital because of physical handicaps or behaviour problems that require medical, nursing or other skills. The local authorities have a statutory duty to provide residential care for all others, and also for those who can leave hospital after a period of treatment there." (para. 158)

and

"In-patient services are needed for those who can no longer remain in the family home or in other residential care and require treatment or training under specialist supervision or constant nursing care. A high proportion will need this because their mental handicap is associated with severe physical disability or behaviour disorder." (para. 180)

The work of Albert Kushlick (Director of the Wessex Health Care Evaluation Research Unit) in setting up homes for mentally handicapped children in the community has proved that multiply handicapped children *can* live in small, locally-based accommodation, and it is unfortunate that the valuable work being done in Wessex has not had more influence on the development of community care for severely handicapped children. It seems that the White Paper, by emphasizing that multiply handicapped children need hospital care, has encouraged local authority administrators to categorise children according to preconceived ideas about their management difficulties; and the two categories which are most likely to jeopardise a handicapped child's chances of living in the community are non-ambulation and incontinence. Uninformed ideas about these two problems are likely to influence initial plans, which are subsequently passed by committees largely composed of members who have little practical knowledge about multiply handicapped children.

The fact that being in a wheelchair diminishes a child's chance of community accommodation would seem contrary to the philosophy of the *Disabled Persons Act*[9], which advocated the adaptation of homes so that non-ambulant adults and children could remain living in the community. It should also be borne in mind that incontinent children do not require the constant attendance of trained nurses. The majority are unlikely to soil themselves more than once or twice a day, and changing a child's pants may be managed efficiently in 10 to 15 minutes if a roomy bathroom and modern aids (such as plastic pants and incontinence pads) are available. There are also excellent training programmes, devised by psychologists, which may help some of these children to become continent.

Of course multiply handicapped children do present many problems and do make great demands on the adults who care for them, but whether the children live at home, in a children's Home or in a hospital, the continuous demands for dealing successfully with their handicaps are the same — adults are needed who have the time and understanding to give secure care, and appropriate aids and modern household facilities are required to help these

9. Department of Health and Social Security (1970) *Chronically Sick and Disabled Persons Act.* London: H.M.S.O.

adults and their children.

Teachers in local special schools

Five of the 223 children in the study went to local special day-schools, but there was virtually no contact between their teachers and the special-care ward staff: only one of the teachers had visited the hospital and talked to the staff of the ward from which the child in her class came each day.

In order to get a picture of what the teachers in local special schools knew about the special-care wards, 16 schools were visited in the areas of the eight hospitals. The teachers had no knowledge about the multiply handicapped children in the mental handicap hospitals. Like administrators in social service departments, they tended to have preconceived ideas about the difficulties of managing children who were very severely multiply handicapped. Even the staff of the special schools which had classes for multiply handicapped children believed that children living in hospital were in need of constant nursing and medical care.

The following situations illustrate the wide gap in understanding between local communities and long-stay hospitals, and also highlight the differences in staffing in local education authority special schools and hospital wards. In Larch Hospital there were 27 children in the special-care ward, commonly looked after by four to five nursing staff, sometimes with only three staff on duty in the evenings and all over the week-ends. These children had no specialist help at all (*i.e.* therapy services). In contrast, four miles away there was a local special day-school which had 19 staff for 38 multiply handicapped children — six non-teaching classroom assistants, five qualified teachers, four NNEB assistants, two physiotherapists, one school nurse and one assistant school nurse.

In another area, the teachers at a special day-school complained that they were kept very busy at lunch time in the school because they had to feed six children; there were two staff to do this, helped by two very able senior pupils. When the teachers were asked what their reactions would be if they were expected to feed 29 children with only four staff, they said that such a thing could not happen anywhere, and that nobody would allow it. One said "if we had that problem the head teacher would ring up the office and help would be sent at once". Those teachers found it impossible to visualise such a problem, yet three miles away from their school, in Birch Hospital's special-care ward, there were indeed usually only four nurses to feed 29 children. The teachers, though working professionally with handicapped children, had no knowledge of the problems facing the handicapped children and staff in Birch Hospital, despite the fact that the hospital served the area in which the school was situated, and if any of the children from the day school had family problems they were likely to be admitted to the hospital for permanent care.

Teachers working with handicapped children in the community need to be better informed of the problems of children in long-stay hospitals, and of the vast differences between the resources and standards in hospitals and those

41

in local education authority establishments. An awareness of these problems might encourage teachers to comment on the deficiencies of institutional care and thus help to influence change.

Members of Community Health Councils

Community Health Councils (CHCs) were set up in 1974, when the National Health Service was reorganised. Their function is to act as spokesmen for the consumers of local health services and to monitor the standard of services, but they have no executive powers. There are 229 CHCs in England and Wales, financed by their Regional Health Authorities. The average annual budget for each CHC is approximately £12,000 to £15,000. Each CHC has between 18 and 33 members, half of whom are appointed by local authorities, at least one-third by local voluntary bodies and the remainder by the Regional Health Authority.

In a postal survey made by the Committee on the Child Health Services[10] which reported in 1976, it was found that between 8 and 15 per cent of CHC members were also members of voluntary organisations connected with children's needs, for example the National Association for the Welfare of Children in Hospital, the National Deaf Children's Society, or the National Society for Mentally Handicapped Children. This finding would suggest that the formation of CHCs would have helped handicapped children in long-stay hospitals, who had not previously had an official local body specifically interested in child welfare to speak for them.

Contact was made with the CHCs connected with the hospitals which were visited in this study, in order to discover their involvement with multiply handicapped children in long-stay hospitals. Each Council had sub-divided itself into 'special interest groups', composed of four to five members who would undertake to look at some special area of health care, for example mental illness, physical handicap, mental handicap, health services for children or health services for the elderly. However, it appeared that by organising themselves into such strictly categorised groups, each of which specialised in *one* particular area of need or handicap, CHC members were not able to monitor the multiplicity of the services needed by handicapped children in institutions. The children had been included in the vague category of 'mental handicap' because they were in mental handicap hospitals, but this meant that the CHC members were not necessarily considering their *needs as children*, nor their needs as *children with physical and/or sensory handicaps*. Those members who had selected as their special interest one of the three categories of physical handicap, mental handicap or children's health services were not sharing knowledge and ideas in order to look broadly at the all-round needs of hospitalised children with multiple handicaps. Indeed, CHC members with an interest in 'mental handicap' seemed to be at a loss when faced with

10. Department of Health and Social Security (1976) *Fit for the Future. Report of the Committee on the Child Health Services*. (Chairman: Professor S. D. M. Court) Cmnd. 6684. London: H.M.S.O.

42

mentally handicapped children who had additional disabilities.

From the reports made by CHC members after visiting their local mental handicap hospitals, it seems that they had little understanding of, or correct information on the problems of handicapped children in institutions. For example, after a visit to Ash Hospital special-care ward, which accommodated 24 multiply handicapped children, the CHC report gave a favourable picture of the ward conditions, and referred especially to "how pleased CHC members were to see the radiogram and large colour television". There was no mention of the fact that the cerebral-palsied children did not have correctly designed tables and chairs and were often fed on the floor.

One Community Health Council had formed a special interest group on 'problems of long-term care', but the chairman of this CHC expressed surprise at my referring to the multiply handicapped children in the special-care ward being deprived of mothering care because of the grave shortage of ward staff. Another Council was shown the new physiotherapy department of a mental handicap hospital, and assumed that the physically disabled children received daily physiotherapy. They did not know that six months earlier the hospital's only physiotherapist had decided that she would no longer give the children any physiotherapy.

The shortcomings that the CHCs had so far shown in respect to the long-stay hospital children appear to have several causes:

(1) Some CHC members were new to National Health Service work; they were overawed by visiting hospital premises and not sure what they were supposed to be looking for.

(2) Some were long-standing members of the hospital's League of Friends, or were former Hospital Management Committee members, and had a rosy and unrealistic picture of 'their' hospital. They knew the hospital very well from the aspects of fund-raising, garden-fetes or small committees, but they did not understand the problems of deprivation which result from children living in long-stay institutions.

(3) On their visits, CHC members were shown around by officers of the hospitals, and much of their knowledge of the hospitals was based on assumptions made on these conducted tours. They rarely got an 'inside' picture of what was happening. For instance, they were perhaps aware that the hospital had a physiotherapy department, an occupational therapy department, a social worker and a speech therapist, but they did not know exactly how much help the children were receiving from those departments.

(4) CHC members had little practical knowledge about handicapped children.

It is unfortunate that the Community Health Councils were failing to grasp the problems of multiply handicapped children in long-stay hospitals, because these children form a very inarticulate group of consumers and especially need an official body of spokesmen — such as a Community Health Council — to be active on their behalf. CHCs might have helped the children by drawing particular attention to:

(a) The children's need for therapy services.

43

(*b*) The children's need to have the same standard of health-care services as is received by ordinary children living in the community, particularly with regard to glasses, hearing-aids, orthopaedic attention and dental care.
(*c*) The fact that understaffing in the wards was affecting standards of child care and depriving the children of mothering attention.
(*d*) The need for more community accommodation to be made available for multiply handicapped children.

Voluntary organisations

Seven of the eight hospitals had a League of Friends, some members of which had handicapped sons or daughters living in the hospitals. Most Leagues kept to their traditional rôle of fund-raising, providing amenities for the wards, and taking responsibility for the Annual Fete, and they avoided developing a pressure-group image. But in one hospital the League had parent members who were seeking to play a part in the management of the hospital.

In seven of the eight hospitals there were also good contacts with local voluntary organisations, such as Rotary Clubs, WRVS, youth clubs and church groups. These groups involved themselves in the hospitals in various ways, for example by fund-raising, organising outings, giving parties, manning the visitors' canteen at week-ends, running evening-clubs, or helping in under-staffed wards, in the adventure playground, or with family transport. Six of the eight hospitals employed a Voluntary Service Organiser to co-ordinate the work of the volunteers. In one hospital nobody was responsible for organising voluntary help (and this hospital had fewer volunteers than any of the other hospitals), and in another a senior nurse was responsible for volunteers. This last hospital had the longest list of contacts with voluntary organisations and the most imaginative ideas about voluntary work; for example, ambulant mentally handicapped adults went to the local comprehensive school in the evenings to use the sports facilities there.

An idea being promoted in two of the hospitals was that each ward was named after a nearby village and was 'adopted' by the village's clubs and organisations. In some cases this had resulted in successful, continuing contacts.

However, even in the hospitals with an impressive list of contacts with local voluntary organisations and a good League of Friends, there was still some difficulty in developing an active voluntary service in the special-care wards. There was little direct contact between the 223 children in the study and any local voluntary organisation. Sometimes the hospitals' Voluntary Service Organiser would allocate small groups of volunteers from a church group or a youth group to one of the special-care wards in order to help with staff shortages and to do routine tasks such as dressing, bathing and feeding, but these volunteers generally seemed unsure of their rôle in the special-care wards. (See pp. 45-47 for further reference to individual volunteers in special-care wards.)

44

There was no contact between the special-care wards and the large national voluntary organisations which have an interest in particular handicaps, such as The Spastics Society, The National Society for Mentally Handicapped Children, The National Deaf Children's Society, or The Royal National Institute for the Blind. It would have been difficult, perhaps, for members of local branches of these organisations to have involved themselves in the hospitals, because many branch-members were themselves parents of handicapped children and were fully occupied in caring for their handicapped children at home and in trying to improve local community services. But these large organisations, which are highly knowledgeable about the needs of children with particular handicaps, might have a great deal to offer multiply handicapped children living in hospitals, through the advice of their professional staff (teachers, therapists, social workers, administrators), who give excellent service to blind, deaf, mentally handicapped and cerebral-palsied children living in the community, through day centres, schools and individual family contact. The extent to which such advice would be welcomed was evident in one hospital which had received a visit from a Regional Educational Adviser of The Royal National Institute for the Blind. This adviser, skilled in assessing and advising on the needs of blind children, had visited the hospital to see a blind baby who was receiving day care, and while there had been asked for advice on one of the blind children living in the special-care ward. She was able to advise on his education and communication needs, and followed this up with a written report for the ward staff and teachers. This advice was greatly appreciated. However, of all the 223 children in this study, that child was the only one to have received the professional advice of a paid officer of one of the national organisations concerned with sensory handicap.

It would be of great value if these large national voluntary organisations, with their special expertise which could be used by hospital staff, were able to develop a policy of fostering definite links with long-stay hospitals through the organisations' regional officers, social workers or educational advisers. Many parents caring for their handicapped children at home have valuable contacts with voluntary organisations, and these contacts should be equally available to ward staff, who are in many cases acting as the children's substitute parents. Advice might be offered on such matters as correct hearing-aids, therapy, language development, visual handicap, special furniture, assessment, and possible placement in community accommodation.

Individual volunteers in the hospitals

There were fewer individual volunteers in the wards for multiply handicapped children than there were in the wards for the more able children. Only three of the 223 children had been 'adopted' by a regular voluntary visitor, one of whom was a retired man who had been taking an interest in a 12-year-old boy ever since he and his wife had visited the hospital on its Open Day. The second was a hospital teacher who visited a 14-year-old boy who had been in her class when he was younger. The third was a 16-year-old schoolgirl who was shortly to begin training as a nursing cadet; she visited a 10-year-old blind boy. These three visitors had been going to the wards two or three times a week, helping with the children's care and taking them out for walks. Although none of the three children could speak, they appeared to respond to these regular visitors by laughter, vocalising and facial expressions, and holding out their hands.

Other regular volunteers in the special-care wards consisted of young people who were still at school, who came in to help the nurses during the week-ends and evenings. In Elm Hospital, three schoolgirls had been working in the special-care ward at week-ends for over a year. One of these worked from 9am until 7pm every Saturday, and was considered to be as reliable as a member of staff. In fact, on several occasions the ward was staffed only by this 15-year-old volunteer and a student nurse. Although these particular volunteers enjoyed giving this service to the wards, using them to supplement shortages of ward staff could be a misuse of volunteers and an encouragement for staff shortages to remain unremedied by the Area Health Authorities.

Apart from these few volunteers who were loyal to particular children or wards, there was some difficulty in getting volunteers for special-care wards. The physical appearance of grossly disabled children sometimes shocked prospective volunteers, and the children's inability to communicate made others feel very uneasy. Some volunteers disliked the mess (*e.g.* dribbling, messy feeding habits) of the children, but some also thought that they received insufficient support from hospital staff: they were often 'thrown in at the deep end', were given no counselling about the ward, and were not given any specific job to do which would have made them feel useful. Some volunteers stood about feeling embarrassed, and even unwelcome.

None of the eight hospitals had a specific policy for organising voluntary work for their special-care wards. If individual volunteers liked the ward or the children they continued to visit, as in the case of the three wards where children had been 'adopted' by volunteers. But this attachment was entirely dependent on the individual volunteers.

Voluntary Service Organisers in hospitals need to give much more support to their volunteers who are going into special-care wards. Some of the volunteers are new to hospitals and feel very upset at seeing multiply handicapped children, so there should be opportunities for them to discuss their worries with the Voluntary Service Organiser. Volunteers in special-care wards need to have their rôle clearly defined. They can be helped to feel that they have a part to play in the ward, either through being attached to one particular child who is without a family (see pp. 17-18), or through working on a project with nurses and other volunteers in the ward. Projects might cover such play activities as water-play, rolling dough, mixing earth, finger- or foot-painting, clapping games, music, going for walks or shopping. Although the children may not be able to participate very actively in such projects, they could enjoy the experiences if the activities were organised on a one-to-one basis by small groups of volunteers working closely together.

Many of the problems which upset volunteers, for example worries about the children's appearance and severe handicaps, might have been eased if the Voluntary Service Organisers themselves had taken more initiative to 'sell' multiply handicapped children to volunteers. But, unfortunately, some Organisers themselves had limited knowledge about handicapped children, and their own attitudes were influenced by their ideas about the unresponsiveness of the children. For example, in one hospital the Voluntary Service Organiser referred to the special-care ward children as "little vegetables" and said that she rarely sent volunteers to their ward "because it wouldn't be fair on the volunteers".

Staff as volunteers

Although this chapter is concerned with what the community knows about children in special-care wards, it would be incomplete if this section on individual volunteers failed to mention the voluntary work done by staff. It was not unusual for nurses, especially students and pupils, to become volunteers when off duty: in fact in every hospital there were one or two nurses who came back to the wards during their free time, and they sometimes brought their non-nursing friends to help with the children, or to take them out for a walk or home to tea with them.

Conclusions regarding community links

(1) Staff in special-care wards appear to be justified in saying that "people outside don't want to know about *these* kids" (p. 39).

(2) Professionals working in the community appear to exaggerate the problems of incontinence and non-ambulation, and there are grave misconceptions about how difficult it is to 'manage' multiply handicapped children in the community.

(3) Teachers working with handicapped children in the community appear to be unaware of the problems facing children and staff in long-stay hospitals.

(4) Community Health Councils, supposedly representing consumers in the National Health Services, are uninformed about the problems of children in long-stay hospitals.

(5) Voluntary organisations which have expert knowledge about particular handicaps are not making that expertise available to help multiply handicapped children in long-stay hospitals.

(6) Potential volunteers are being lost to special-care wards because of lack of support from the Voluntary Service Organisers in hospitals.

RECOMMENDATIONS

(1) Professionals working with handicapped children in the community, *i.e.* in education, health care, residential care, social work and social service administration, should find out about the problems of handicapped children in long-stay hospitals.

(2) Community Health Councils should regard all children in long-stay hospitals as being in special need of an effective body of spokesmen because they have problems which are caused not only by their handicaps but also by their deprivation of family life. Community Health Councils might educate themselves about the needs of these children by: (*a*) visiting other residential premises (*e.g.* children's Homes and boarding schools); (*b*) inviting to their meetings speakers who have experience of handicapped children and residential care; (*c*) co-opting onto the Community Health Council people who have some special knowledge or experience about handicapped children and residential care; (*d*) organising seminars for themselves, the public and the staff about the needs of handicapped children.

(3) Voluntary organisations with special knowledge about some particular handicap should endeavour to make contact with long-stay hospitals and share that expertise. Perhaps the large national voluntary organisations could each appoint their own hospital liaison officers to foster such contacts.

(4) Individual volunteers in hospitals should receive more support from the hospital's Voluntary Service Organisers. The organisers themselves should be better informed about the needs and abilities of multiply handicapped children.

CHAPTER 5

The Hospital Schools

Introduction

The 1970 Education (Handicapped Children) Act[11], which came into effect in April 1971, made the Department of Education and Science responsible for the education of all handicapped children. Before that time, children who had been classified as severely mentally subnormal had not been the responsibility of local education authorities and had not attended local education authority special schools, but had been offered places at junior training centres. These centres were run by the local health and welfare committees until the Seebohm Report of 1968[12], and by the local authority social service departments from 1968 until the Education Act of 1970.

Some junior training centres were excellent, and many of the staff (whether qualified or not) were very experienced in helping severely mentally handicapped children. However, other centres were in very poor premises, resources and equipment were lacking, and the staff were not well qualified to work with handicapped children. Many centres were in prefabricated huts or run-down village halls, and they did not accept non-ambulant children because there were no facilities for changing or washing multiply handicapped children and there was no room for wheelchairs. This meant that in some areas the parents of multiply handicapped children had their children at home with them the whole time.

The Education Act was greeted with relief by most people, especially by parents, for it meant that all severely mentally handicapped children would have the benefits of local authority special education services. The transfer to the local education authorities resulted in some remarkably swift changes: within five years new premises were being built to replace the older centres, more money was made available for equipment, there was an increase in qualified staff, more opportunities for staff training, and provision was made for 'special-care children', *i.e.* non-ambulant children with multiple handicaps. It is to the credit of many local education authorities that they did all they could to bring the facilities for severely mentally handicapped children up to the same standard as those being offered to other categories of handicapped children in special day-schools. However, some authorities have been slower than others in making radical improvements, and conditions in those areas for staff and children are still difficult.

11. Department of Education and Science (1970) *Education (Handicapped Children) Act*. London: H.M.S.O.
12. Seebohm Report (1968) *Report of the Committee on Local Authority and Allied Personal Social Services.* (Chairman: Baron Seebohm.) London: H.M.S.O.

After the 1970 Act, the former junior training centres were classified as ESN (Severe) Schools, while the original ESN Schools (which had always catered for children with milder mental handicaps) were re-named ESN (Mild) Schools. Needless to say, there has been some heated discussion about the status that these two classifications confer on the schools, and the inevitable result has been that the teachers and children in ESN(M) Schools are considered to be higher in the intellectual pecking order than the teachers and children in ESN(S) Schools. Parents also are made to feel that their children are 'getting on' if they are transferred from a 'severe' to a 'mild' school.

The Education Act and mental handicap hospital schools

Mental handicap hospitals have always had schools on the premises. Some were built more than 50 years ago, often of a similar design to a small village school and quite inappropriate for physically disabled children. Children with multiple handicaps generally stayed in their wards and received no education or occupation. The majority of teachers in hospital schools were unqualified and often had to work in poor conditions, with inadequate stock and a lack of in-service training. However, like the staff of junior training centres in the community, many were experienced in helping severely mentally handicapped children.

Prior to the 1970 Education Act, all mental handicap hospital schools were managed by the hospital Management Committee, but after the Act they became the responsibility of local education authorities. They were then classified as ESN(S) special schools, and the teachers were employed by the local education authority. The same improvements then began to be made in them as were being made in junior training centres; qualified staff were gradually employed, premises were improved if necessary and more money was available for equipment.

Some head teachers in hospital schools had long-standing poor relationships with other departments in the hospital and with the hospital Management Committees and made the Education Act an excuse to completely separate the school from the rest of the hospital. However, others who enjoyed good relationships with other hospital staff regarded the Education Act as a means of gaining advantages for the children; they have appreciated the improvements that have been possible through coming under the local education authorities, but they have not separated their schools from the rest of the hospital.

Special-care ward children and the Education Act

Although the 1970 Education Act appears to have been a workable piece of legislation for severely mentally handicapped children living in the community, it has not been so straightforward for multiply handicapped children living in special-care wards of long-stay hospitals. They comprise the most severely handicapped group of children to be found anywhere*, and there has always been some confusion about what education can actually mean for them. The Education Act has done little to clarify this confusion, merely saying that local education authorities were now to be responsible for the education of all children, however handicapped, and the Department of Education and Science (DES) has made no firm statement about their needs.

In 1975, the DES issued a very useful booklet[13] which is essentially practical, offers a host of helpful suggestions, and stresses the need for setting objectives in the teaching of mentally handicapped children. Anybody working with such children would do well to read this booklet, and it is an excellent introduction to teachers entering special education. However, the booklet is particularly disappointing in its references to multiply handicapped children in hospital. Only two of its 73 pages are given to any discussion of their educational problems, and it seems to assume that if children are in hospital they will be receiving diagnosis and treatment. For example:

'Gradually those children who need only residential care will move into community homes and the role of the hospital will focus more sharply on diagnosis and assessment, perhaps over a long period, and on residential treatment for those children whose handicaps and behaviour require the range of special services in a hospital. The hospital population is a more severely handicapped one and will become increasingly so. The proportion of profoundly handicapped children is likely to increase, as will that of hyperactive and disturbed children.' (p. 59/60)

Another unsatisfactory aspect of the booklet is that it tends to bracket together the children who have multiple physical handicaps and those who have behaviour disorders, and it does not distinguish adequately the differing needs of either group, nor define any clear educational objectives for them. For example, in the chapter entitled 'Educating the Most Severely Handicapped Children', it is stated:

'In the day schools there has been a tradition that one part of the school should be designed for children whose behaviour or associated physical

*A 1977 survey, conducted by Dr. Gordon A. Bland, showed the disabilities affecting students in some mental handicap hospital schools to be as follows: —

	No. of schools	No. of students in sample	Students affected	
			No.	%
Severe physical handicap (incl. non-ambulant)	47	3454	1051	30.4
Severe speech defects (incl. lack of speech)	47	3462	2745	79.3
Serious visual defects (excl. total blindness)	48	3554	301	8.47
Blind	48	3554	125	3.5
Serious hearing defects	48	3554	265	7.46

13. Department of Education and Science (1975) *Educating Mentally Handicapped Children. Education pamphlet No. 60.* London: H.M.S.O.

handicaps make them difficult to educate with other class groups. Similarly in hospitals some children attend school while others remain in the wards or receive some treatment elsewhere. It is now the duty of local education authorities to provide education for all children irrespective of the degree of their handicap. The education programme must provide for the most severely handicapped, whether in school or hospital, and this presents a challenge to ingenuity and inventiveness.'

'The children concerned tend to form two sub-groups: those who may be hyperactive, aggressive, self-destructive and who have psychotic features in their behaviour; and those with multiple physical handicaps. Both groups may be incontinent, unable to feed themselves and unable to communicate.' (p. 31)

It is to be hoped that the DES may now be able to issue a further pamphlet which will look in more detail at the particular problems of multiply handicapped children in special-care wards of long-stay hospitals.

A conventional education, which concentrates on achieving skills in reading, writing and number understanding, would appear to be of little value to very severely multiply handicapped children. Some of them have such meagre abilities in their hands, their sight and their movements that they may seem unable to derive much obvious benefit even from a good nursery-school environment; and some make so little response that the teachers wonder if they are even *aware* of their surroundings. The doubts that many teachers have of ever being able to teach anything to such children, coupled with a lack of information about what to do with children who seem unable to play, has led some hospital head-teachers to exclude the most severely disabled of the special-care ward children from the school altogether, although the Education Act states clearly that they were now the educational responsibility of the local education authority.

This chapter discusses the education being received by the school-age children in this study (see also Table III).

How decisions were taken about education

The decision to offer a child only part-time education, or to exclude him altogether, ultimately rested with the head teacher in each of the hospital schools, although occasionally the decision was taken in conjunction with the nurse in charge of the ward. The most common reasons for excluding children from school were: (a) the child would not 'respond'; (b) the child was noisy (i.e. given to moaning, crying, giggling or shouting); (c) the school premises were not suitable (e.g. no room for a very large, helpless child in a wheelchair); and (d) the child was too physically disabled to benefit from school.

The school at Bay Hospital excluded more children than any other hospital school in the study. 20 children in the main special-care ward (Ward 2) were aged between five and 15 years, but only two attended school full-time. Eight more attended school for one hour each day, another went to school only

TABLE III

Education being received by the 153 children aged between 5 and 15 years

Hospital	No. children 5-15 years	No. receiving full-time education	No. receiving part-time education*	Total receiving some education	Total receiving no education	Where education was taking place: Hospital school building	Wards	Room adjoining wards	Special schools in community†
Ash	18	18	—	18	—	18 FT	—	—	—
Bay: Ward 2	20	2	9	11	9	2 FT, 9 PT	—	—	—
Other	9	2	4	6	3	2 FT, 4 PT	—	—	—
Birch	14	14	—	14	—	—	—	14 FT	—
Elm	12	2	9	11	1	2 FT, 9 PT	—	—	—
Larch	24	21	—	21	3	20 FT	—	—	1 FT
Oak: Ward 7 + others	26	10	14	24	2	10 FT, 11 PT	3 PT	—	—
Willows	5	5	—	5	—	5 FT ‡	—	—	—
Pine: Ward 10	11	10	1	11	—	7 FT	1 PT	—	3 FT
Other	14	6	8	14	—	3 FT, 1 PT	8 PT	—	1 FT, 1 PT
TOTALS	153	90	45	135	18	69 FT, 34 PT	12 PT	14 FT	5 FT, 1 PT

*Part-time indicates perhaps every morning in school, or perhaps an hour a day, or a teacher occasionally visiting the ward.

† The six children attending community special schools had been selected as most likely to benefit from them. Five were ambulant, with good hand ability and some speech; the sixth was a non-ambulant, speechless, cerebral-palsied girl with no hand ability, who attended part-time to learn how to use a 'Possum' machine.

‡ School was situated just outside hospital grounds.

during the mornings, and the remaining nine were excluded altogether. Between them, these 20 children were legally entitled to receive a total of 500 hours of education a week, whereas their total amounted to only 102 hours. Because of the shortage of ward staff and a general lack of guidance about play activities, the children who did not go to school at all, or went only part-time, usually just sat about the ward doing nothing.

The procedure for getting a child into Bay Hospital school was that the sister of the special-care ward applied to the head teacher, who then arranged for his senior teacher to visit the ward and 'test' the child. The senior teacher explained to me that in order to test the child's suitability for education she usually took her bunch of keys to the ward and rattled them in front of the child's face; she also tickled the child, stroked his face and spoke to him. If there was any response (*i.e.* if he smiled or turned his head or made eye contact), she might recommend that the child should go to school. She said she only needed to spend half an hour in a ward to assess whether a child could benefit from education. This 'selection' procedure stemmed from the philosphy that handicapped children should meet a certain standard, loosely based on traditional school-teaching methods, which was imposed by the hospital school. The result would seem to be a violation of the Education Act.

The exclusion of so many children from the Bay Hospital school was even more disquieting because this school had the most palatial premises of any in the eight hospitals. It had been specially designed, with long sloping corridors to the upper floors to enable easy access for wheelchairs, and it was sited close to the children's wards. There were 25 teachers, a full-time school secretary and three classroom assistants for approximately 150 children (21 of the children came daily from the community). One teacher was unqualified, but the other 24 had ordinary teaching diplomas and/or degrees and diplomas in the education of handicapped children.

Ash Hospital School, in complete contrast, had very poor premises, but all 18 school-age children in the special-care ward were accepted full-time, regardless of their severe disabilities; they even received their lunch in the school.

Hospital school teachers and their children's lunch-time

The teachers in Ash Hospital School were the only hospital teachers who were giving the children their lunch in school. The organisation of the lunches might have been criticised for being unhygienic because the facilities were very inadequate, the meal being served and eaten in a very congested classroom in which children were sometimes also changed and washed. However, the hospital teachers believed that the children should stay at school for their lunch in the same way as ordinary children have lunch at school; they regarded the lunch-hour as an aspect of the children's social learning.

In two of the other hospitals some of the teachers went to the wards and helped to feed the children. For example, in Larch Hospital a teacher and three classroom assistants helped to feed four of the special-care children every lunch-time. They were encouraging the four children to hold their own spoons, and the teacher hoped that they would eventually learn to feed themselves. However, the manner in which the teacher and her assistants were able to feed the children at lunch-time (patiently waiting for them to lift the spoons to their mouths) was not possible at breakfast-time or supper-time, nor at any meal-times during the week-ends or school holidays, because the shortage of ward staff prevented the children from receiving the one-to-one attention they needed.

Hospital school premises

Three of the hospital schools had poor school premises, with no special facilities for physically disabled children and with inconvenient washing and changing facilities. Another three of the schools had adequate premises, having originally been built as hospital schools and since enlarged.

Bay Hospital School had been purpose-built in the 1960s and had every facility, including a large, pleasant recreation hall, cookery and craft rooms, and comfortable staff-rooms and offices.

Willows Hospital school was built on land immediately adjoining the hospital grounds but actually off hospital property altogether. On the same site as the school there was a social services adult training centre, and an adult hostel. The school was new and well-designed. 84 of the children at the school came from the community and 28 from the hospital. The head teacher was emphatic about keeping the school entirely separate from the hospital, and although nurses escorted the children from the wards to the school and back again, they were discouraged from entering the children's classrooms and taking an interest in their education.

Transporting the children to school

The six children who went to special day-schools in the community were taken by taxi or hospital bus, usually without complications. The 103 children who attended schools in the hospitals (or, as in Willows, adjoining the hospital) got there and back either by teachers, classroom assistants and nurses pushing them in wheelchairs, large prams or baby-buggies, or they were picked up by a small hospital bus, with nurses, teachers or classroom assistants acting as escorts.

There were occasional difficulties about getting the children to and from the wards and the hospital schools, sometimes caused by the children's severe handicaps (*i.e.* they were awkward to lift into the bus), by shortages of wheelchairs, bad weather or shortages of ward staff and school staff, or by a breakdown of the bus or its delegation to other duties in the hospital.

Hospital teachers are not officially required to escort children to and from wards and school, but some did so because they regarded escort work as part of the educational service that they were giving the children. In Bay Hospital, however, the teachers made a point of never pushing the children to and from school, which caused considerable inconvenience to the special-care ward nurses whose numbers were depleted when they had to leave the ward and take children to the school. This particular ward had 26 long-term multiply handicapped children in it, of whom 20 were under 16 years of age. Only two of the children were receiving full-time education, but nine more were having part-time education (see pp. 52-54), which meant that if only four nurses were on duty and two had to keep running between the school and the ward acting as escorts, then only two nurses were left on the ward with at least 15 children for a lot of the time between 9.15 and 11.45am and between 1.15 and 3.30pm. In these circumstances it was difficult for the nurses to organise a sustained programme of play activities in the ward, so it meant that the children were neither getting the education to which they were entitled nor any playgroup on the ward.

Problems in getting the children to school

Because of the disorganised arrangements for getting children from the ward to the hospital school, they often arrived late. In Elm Hospital, for example, a group of day-children came by taxi from their homes 10 miles away and usually arrived at the hospital school promptly at 9.30am. In contrast, children coming from the special-care ward (less than 300 yards from the school) were often between 30 and 40 minutes late in the morning and 25 minutes late in the afternoon. Apart from the general inconvenience, this meant that each child was likely to lose approximately one hour of education each day.

The main causes of this lateness were shortages of ward staff, and the hospital bus being delayed or sent on some other errand around the hospital. The lateness was irritating to the teachers because it meant that the children missed so much school-time, but their irritation tended to be directed more at individual members of the ward staff than at the poor organisation of hospital care which resulted in shortages of ward staff at essential times in the morning.

In some of the hospitals the problem of lateness was also coupled with that of children arriving in school badly dressed — perhaps wearing another child's clothes, with their shoes on the wrong feet, in summer dresses on cold days and in warm jumpers on hot days, minus a vest or wearing two vests, or with odd shoes and socks on. This seeming evidence of poor care angered some of the teachers, but had they seen the situation in some of the wards between 7.15am and 9.15am they might have understood a little more why the children arrived in school late and dressed in the wrong clothes. For example, in some special-care wards there were only two staff on duty at 7.15am to start getting 20 or 25 totally disabled children out of bed. At 7.30am another two staff would probably come on duty, but it was very likely that three of these four nurses did not know the children because they were new students, new nursing assistants, or relief nurses sent from other wards. After feeding, washing and dressing the children, the nurses then had to put them in outdoor clothes, find safe wheelchairs for them and have them ready for going to school by 9.15am.

Starting at 7.30am and working at top speed, it was not an impossible task for four nurses to accomplish all this by 9.15am, but the pace at which it had to be done would leave no time to check the children's clothes, or on their hair-brushing, teeth-cleaning, and general appearance. The fact that some of the nurses might not know the names of the children made it very easy for a child to be dressed in the wrong clothes.

Relationships between teachers and nurses

The relationships between teachers and nurses varied between the eight hospitals. In Bay Hospital the teachers appeared to have a somewhat arrogant attitude towards the nurses, which was largely influenced by the head teacher who had no sympathy for nurses, and the nurses seemed to be very timid of the teachers. In other hospitals bad relationships between teachers and nurses took the form of deliberate coolness: for example, if information had to be exchanged they sent each other curt notes rather than visiting one another's premises. In some hospitals there were arguments between nurses and teachers about such matters as school or ward outings, children eating sweets in school and being sick when they got back to the ward, children being sent back to the wards with paint on their clothes or sand in their shoes, and children being sent to school when they were obviously not very well.

Bad relationships between school and ward staff appeared to be caused mainly because neither group was familiar with the work or the problems of the other. In two of the hospital schools the teachers of the children from the special-care wards had been working in the school for over a year but had never visited the special-care wards or introduced themselves to the children's nurses. During my hospital visits, which took me into the hospital schools as well as into the wards, teachers would sometimes say to me: "Could you let the nurses know the sort of things we are doing with the children in school", while the nurses would say: "You can let the teachers know our difficulties when we haven't got enough staff." Both groups seemed to be reluctant to visit each other's premises to discuss their work.

In Ash Hospital there were good relationships between teachers and nurses because they frequently visited each other's premises, and there was a reciprocation of services between both groups: for example, the teachers always went to the ward at 9am and helped to get the children ready for school, then they took all 18 school-age children up to the school themselves and kept them there until 3.30pm, when they took them back to the wards themselves. The nurses went to the school and helped with mid-morning drinks, and offered their help as extra 'pushers' if the teachers were taking the children on an outing.

The *place* where the teachers worked had a significant influence on the relationship between nurses and teachers. In Birch Hospital, where the schoolroom adjoined the special-care ward, nurses and teachers enjoyed good relationships because they saw each other every day, hung their coats up together, had coffee together, and gave the children their mid-morning and mid-afternoon drinks together. Nurses often went into the schoolroom to see

57

what the children were doing, and they were familiar with the teachers' aims.

The teachers usually had better relationships with student nurses than they had with qualified nurses or nursing assistants. This was probably because during their training some student nurses did a six-weeks placement in the hospital school. They enjoyed this contact with the children in the school, and those who were making a study of a particular child were glad of the opportunity to see 'their child' out of the ward environment. The teachers also were generally quite helpful in giving the student nurses access to the children's school records and assessment charts.

However, although the children's school records were made available to student nurses and nursing staff, teachers did not always have access to the children's medical records. In some hospitals teachers were never allowed to read the children's case-notes, although the information they contained might have been helpful. This emphasis on the confidentiality of medical records was a source of annoyance to teachers, who considered it a slight on their professional integrity.

Some nurses thought that the teachers worked short hours and had long holidays, but perhaps did not realise that some teachers continued to work in their classrooms after the children had gone back to the wards (writing reports, sorting or making apparatus, tidying the rooms), and used part of their holidays for attending conferences and in-service training courses or for running holiday activities for children. Nurses and teachers were sometimes sensitive about what they each thought the others were saying about their work. Some teachers believed that nurses were saying "anyone can play with the children", and some nurses thought that teachers believed "nurses are only good at wiping bottoms". These ideas were expressed in some hospitals, but in others teachers spoke with admiration of the ward staff's work and sympathised with their long hours, while some nurses spoke well of teachers for "trying to get through" to such handicapped children.

A few nurses did have very little faith in what the teachers were doing with the children and thought it "a waste of public money to employ qualified teachers for these children", but this opinion reflected the very low expectations these nurses themselves had of the children and their lack of knowledge about how educational principles might be used to encourage movement and communication and prevent stagnation or regression.

Teachers' relationships with other hospital staff

The teachers of the special-care children had little contact with social workers, voluntary service organisers, doctors or psychologists. However, in Birch Hospital, the teachers had very amicable relationships with the physio-therapists because the special-care children received regular physiotherapy. The therapists worked in the schoolroom adjoining the special-care ward, and this meant that the physiotherapists, nurses and teachers knew each other and got on well together. This suggests that if multiply handicapped children are to get the best out of the hospital services, it is necessary for therapists, teachers and nurses to work together on the same premises as much as possible. If children are taken away to other departments to attend school and physiotherapy, these are likely to be regarded as separate entities—as something *done* to the child for a little while somewhere else—rather than being parts of a continuous way of life. Another result is that one discipline feels the others are letting them down because they are not familiar with each other's work: for example teachers and nurses will fail to sit the children correctly if they do not actually see how a physiotherapist works. There can be no really successful help for the children until there is understanding between all disciplines, and there can be very little understanding until the various disciplines have some practical familiarity with the work that they are all doing.

School holidays

The long school-holidays appeared to cause considerable irritation among all disciplines of hospital staff. In some hospitals the teachers were described as being "just part-time workers", and doctors, nurses and therapists occasionally contended that, if teachers did not stagger their holidays, the children were 'dumped' back in the wards for 12 weeks of the year with nothing to do.

Seven of the eight hospital schools were shut for four weeks in August and had the other usual holidays throughout the year. Only Ash Hospital school had staggered holidays: it closed for two weeks at Easter and two at Christmas, but at no other time. However, it was not evident that these staggered holidays *were* beneficial to the children; in fact they seemed actually to cause problems for the children. One problem was that some members of school staff were always absent, taking their allocation of holiday time, and this meant a dilution in staff, with doubling-up of classes, and teachers standing in for each other. The teachers found this tiring and frustrating because the children were not always happy with the change of teachers, and the teachers themselves were not always happy about colleagues taking over their rooms and their children. Another problem was that the children were said to get 'stale' because of coming to school all the year round, except for two weeks at Easter and two at Christmas. This latter is the more serious problem: children living at home or in residential homes in the community do not go to school all the year round, and the fact that there seemed to be little else to do with these children but send them to school every day reflects a poor standard of child care (and poor staffing) in the wards, resulting in a lack of mothering and suitable activities for the children.

If it is agreed that education should be a means of developing fuller lives for these children, and not merely a matter of moving them to other premises from 9.30am to 3.30pm, it would seem that far more radical changes are needed in the approach to education in hospitals than merely staggering school holidays. For example, should changes be made in the teachers' *hours* of work, their *place* of working and the *content* of their work? Should they work in the evenings instead of during the day: developing play activities and putting the children to bed? Should they perhaps work entirely in the ward and not have a separate school building? Changes such as staggering school holidays distract attention from much wider questions of the children's educational needs, the main one being what responsibility should hospital teachers have in the important issue of child-care practices in long-stay hospitals? The style of life of children in boarding schools for handicapped children is strongly influenced by the teaching staff, but this does not happen in long-stay hospitals because teachers have no responsibility for what happens to the children after school and during week-ends.

What the children did in school

As mentioned earlier (pp. 51-52), there is general confusion about what education actually means for special-care children. When the teachers were asked what their aims were for the children, the most common answer was "to stimulate them". Through stimulation, the teachers hoped to provoke responses which would then lead the children on to some recognisable pattern of nursery-school play.

This 'stimulation' covered a multitude of theories and practices. The most common practice was to lay the child on a mattress underneath a conglomeration of objects dangling from a net or a frame made of coat-hangers. Just above the child's head would dangle painted cotton-reels, balloons, shiny tins, bits of silk, fur or tin-foil, squeaky toys, bells and dolls. These colourful arrays were eye-catching and it was hoped they would attract the attention of the child. Sometimes the child would be encouraged to reach up and catch hold of an object and thus set the whole array bouncing about. When this happened the child would sometimes smile or make sounds. Other forms of stimulation were sitting the children at a tray of water or sand, and trying to encourage them to dangle their hands in it; sitting them at tables with lumps of dough in front of them and encouraging them to prod the dough with their fingers; and sometimes finger-painting or foot-painting. In one special-care classroom there was a dark corner where the children were laid beneath a table covered with a black cloth, and some 'disco' lights fitted under the table twinkled on and off for them. Another classroom had part of the floor built up with mattresses so that children could lie up on them and look out of the windows, which they could not do in their wards. Some classrooms had hammocks and swings in them, to give the children a sense of movement. Many of the special-care classrooms had non-stop music, partly to stimulate the children and partly to alleviate the loneliness that the staff felt because of the children's lack of speech.

The nursery-school type of achievements seen amongst the 129 children who were on the hospital schools' registers were: holding a crayon and scribbling; holding a paint brush and daubing paint; holding a stick and banging a drum or xylophone; filling a pot with sand or water from another pot; emptying sand or water out of a pot; pouring water; saying the first line of a nursery rhyme; putting some bricks into a box; taking bricks out of a box;

doing a small nursery puzzle of three or four inset pieces; and matching four colours. Several, or all, of these activities were achieved by 30 of the children. These were the most able children, with good hand ability. The achievements of the other children were very meagre indeed; in some cases the teachers merely laid the children under the dangling toys, or on the classroom floor with bells tied to their wrists in the hope that they would move and make the bells ring.

Some teachers, seemingly in desperation at not knowing what to do with the children, resorted to fringe 'nursing' duties, and in some of the special-care classes the children spent a considerable amount of time being potted and changed. In two of the hospital schools the children were potted as soon as they arrived, remaining on their pots on the classroom floor for periods of 25 to 40 minutes. Just before lunch they were potted again for a period of 10 minutes, and the same procedure was gone through at the beginning and end of afternoon school. All this potting took up at least an hour of school-time every day, and since many of the children also spent lengthy periods sitting on pots when they were in their wards, its value was very dubious. With the potting in school *and* in the wards, some children were actually spending at least three hours each day sitting on pots. And they were still not pot-trained.

Sitting the children on pots had become a habitual routine for staff to perform, but for the children it was neither educational nor physically comfortable. Teachers and nurses need to discuss and reappraise the purpose of so much potting, for it seems unwise to continue any procedure unless it is known to benefit the children.

The following observations illustrate what some of the children were doing in their hospital schools.

Katherine

Thirteen-year-old Katherine had been in the hospital since she was seven; she was partially sighted, speechless and non-ambulant. She had no grasp ability in her hands, and her body was very stiff.

2pm: Katherine arrived in school and was laid on the floor, alongside a table which had been laid on its side. Tied to the legs of the table were chiffon scarves, bells and pieces of furry material. The idea was that Katherine should feel these bits of material as they hung near her face. The teacher tickled her feet, tickled her under the arms, turned on an alarm-clock beside her, and then threw a brightly-coloured scarf over her face: Katherine lifted her hand and pushed the scarf off her face. The teacher moved to another child. There were three children and one teacher in the schoolroom for this session.

2.15-2.45: Katherine was still in the same position, lying motionless.

2.45: Katherine was moved by the teacher, and laid on her stomach over a foam-rubber wedge, with her hands placed forward in a trough of autumn leaves. It was hoped that she would feel these leaves and "get something from them".

61

3.10: Katherine nose-dived off the wedge and fell into the trough of leaves. The teacher lifted her out, and put her back under the table again. A chiffon scarf hung down near her face.

3.25: The children were taken back to the ward.

During Katherine's 85 minutes in school the teacher had spent 10 minutes in personal contact with her. This afternoon in school was typical of what Katherine did there on other afternoons.

In Katherine's hospital school there were three teachers who worked all the time with multiply handicapped children. Each teacher worked in a separate room and the children came in small groups of three or four at a time for an afternoon or a morning. The three teachers shared one classroom helper: this meant that a teacher would sometimes have a helper for an hour, but would work on her own for a greater part of the day. They said that they felt depressed about their work, they had little job-satisfaction and, having little contact with their own school staff or with the ward staff, they found it lonely to be shut up all day with non-speaking, unresponsive children. They felt they received very little support in their work with multiply handicapped children because the head teacher and the other school staff were more interested in ambulant children who could show some obvious progress.

The teachers said that as well as needing some moral support, they also needed practical support. For example they felt that if they could take the children out on short journeys it might stimulate them, but they were only allowed to use the school bus for two trips a year. They had also asked the head teacher if they could join up together and do physical education activities in the Hall, or go into the cookery or pottery rooms, but there was a general feeling throughout the school that the multiply handicapped children could not benefit from the physical education apparatus or the cookery and pottery facilities. Lacking encouragement to experiment, these isolated special-care class teachers were falling back on sterile attempts to stimulate the children by dangling objects over their heads.

It is understandable that teachers of multiply handicapped children become depressed unless they get support from other staff in the school and encouragement to experiment with group activities.

Eden

Fifteen-year-old Eden had been in hospital for 12 years. He is cerebral-palsied, non-ambulant and speechless, but has good grasp ability in his hands. He attended his hospital school for one hour a day.

1.20: Eden arrived in his classroom. He was lifted out of his wheelchair and laid on the floor. There was one teacher, who had Eden and three ambulant children from another ward. Eden lay on the floor, sucking his hand. In the classroom there was a physiotherapy roll in the middle of the floor, a rocker boat, a dry water-tray, an armchair, three tables pushed to the edge of the room, and four kitchen-type chairs. There was also a 'Wendy' house which was packed tight with a sand-tray and various pieces of broken and unused equipment. The teacher said "the sand tray is always kept in the 'Wendy' house, otherwise the children would get at it and sit in it or throw sand. I have to keep it out of their way". One of the boys, aged about 12, picked up an empty 'Play-doh' tin, looked at it, and then crouched down and banged the tin on the floor. The two other ambulant children roamed about the room. Now and again they sat on the windowsills and banged the windows or the walls with their fists. The teacher sat on the physiotherapy roll, watching them.

1.50: The teacher lifted Eden from the floor where he had been since arriving at 1.20. She placed him astride the roll, sat behind him and held him there for three minutes. Then she put him back on the floor and resumed watching the children, still sitting astride the roll herself.

1.55: Eden dragged himself on his back across the room a little way, then lay still, arching his back and sucking his hand. Being near a cupboard now, he stretched out his hand and shut the cupboard door. The teacher saw him do this and remarked: "Old Eden likes to shut the door". He continued to lie on his back, sucking his hand, until 2.25.

2.25: Eden was lifted into his wheelchair and put by the door, ready to be taken back to the ward. He still sucked his hand.

2.40: Eden was collected by one of the nurses.

The special-care class in Larch Hospital school was in complete contrast to the classes in the other hospital schools attended by Katherine and Eden. In Larch Hospital 15 of the multiply handicapped children were accommodated in one classroom, and all attended full-time. The room was **very** small and cramped: it contained a small swing, two 'Cell Barnes' chairs, bean-bags, small tables and chairs, a three-cornered chair, a large ordinary household bath, pictures, plants, soft toys and two baby-walkers. A cupboard had been pulled across one corner to make a separate division, and here there was a large vibrating mattress on which some of the children liked to lie. A thick yellow carpet was on the floor. Across one corner was a net with mobiles and toys dangling from it, but the children were not left underneath these hanging objects unless they showed an interest in them.

There was one teacher, two full-time assistants and one part-time assistant. The teacher had a diploma in the education of mentally handicapped children, and had previously worked in a junior training centre and then an ESN(S) school in the community. She had been working in Larch Hospital school for less than one year. The part-time classroom assistant was a qualified teacher with a degree in psychology; he worked every afternoon in the class. One of the full-time classroom assistants was unqualified; the other had a nursing qualification and had previously worked in day-nurseries.

The head teacher of Larch Hospital school was very supportive of the special-care group, and gave special attention to these children and their staff in an effort to formulate some philosophy of education for multiply handicapped children. The teacher had a special salary allowance for the responsibility of being in charge of this class.

The teacher said that her aims for the children were still difficult to define, but basically they were to keep them moving and to use any ability they had in order to try and make them more lively. She believed it was important to give the children as much human contact as possible (cuddling, touching) and to try and elicit some response from them through any means that appealed to them as individuals.

It was obvious that the class staff knew the children very well as individuals. Each child had been carefully observed and when the staff described a child they did not merely say "he does not respond", but listed what he *did* respond to and gave details of his abilities, even if they were meagre. By looking all the time at the positive aspects of the children, the staff appeared to be developing a very hopeful approach to their work. They attached great importance to moving the children and changing their positions. They were knelt up, sat cross-legged, put at small tables or into the swing, laid on the vibrating mattress, encouraged to roll, had their arms and legs pulled and their fingers uncurled, and they were encouraged to lift their heads and look about. Sometimes they were put into the bath and helped to stretch and splash and to kick at floating toys. And they were constantly talked to.

Following is a description of 15 minutes in the class. It was a difficult time because the teacher had been left alone with 15 children because the assistants had gone to a rehearsal of the Christmas play, but these 15 minutes illustrate how this teacher was so in tune with her children as individuals that she did not seem to find it a great strain being suddenly left alone with 15 multiply handicapped children, but carried on trying to give them a good service.

The teacher (W.) put Florence in the baby-walker, to stand by a cupboard full of toys. W. encouraged Florence to pull the toys out of the cupboard, but Florence waved her hands into the cupboard and was not very successful in scooping out any toys. W. then went to Ronald, sitting on a chair by the bath, who had a few toys floating in the water. His hands were in the water, and W. tried to help him find his toys in the bath and push them up and down, making waves in the water.

Then she said: "I'll put Henry's favourite record on", found the record and put it on, and Henry turned his head and smiled as he heard the tune start. He was partially sighted. W. sat on the floor and cuddled Herbert. Next she went to Justin and gave him a quick romp, lasting one minute. Then she sat down in front of Henry, held his hands and played with him in time to the music. Next she put Henry on the floor between her knees and exercised his legs.

Whenever W. moved about the room she talked to the children, and, the room being so small, she was able to remain in good contact with them all. As she cuddled and exercised Henry she also kept a hand on nearby Philip, who had a tambourine in his hand. W. shook this towards Henry and made him smile.

64

Henry was then put into a piece of shaped foam-rubber, and W. fetched Caroline from a bean-bag and put her into a small chair, astride it back to front, telling her to hold on to the back. Caroline was partially sighted, but had good grasp ability.

Leonard was put into a new position, kneeling, and his fingers were uncurled. Again Henry was picked up and was carried about the room and talked to. Then W. put him onto a mat, propped up against a bean-bag. Leonard had his kneeling position checked and corrected because he had started to subside (he did not like kneeling). Caroline fell off her chair, onto a pillow lying beside her. She cried very loudly, and W. picked her up, comforted her and put her onto another chair. Then she went to three children who were lying on or near the vibrating mattress in the corner of the room. She said: "I've missed you little lot this afternoon, sorry about that", and briefly touched each of the three children. It was then 3pm and the other staff returned.

This teacher, even when left on her own for a quarter of an hour with 15 children, tried to follow a programme of movement and attention-giving; she contacted 11 of the 15 children, and the attention she gave them, although brief, was warm and individual. The quality of the attention her children received in the 15 minutes was far richer than Katherine and Eden had received from their teachers during more than an hour in a small group of only three to four children.

Although the Larch Hospital school special-care children were just as severely handicapped as those in the other hospital schools, they were lively and noisy, wriggling, kicking and shouting. And although they could not speak, it could not be said that there was a lack of communication in the room, for there was a sense of contact all the time because the staff were so much in touch with the children. The staff were also aware of *how the children reacted to each other*; this was the only special-care class in any of the schools where the children were deliberately placed together and encouraged to touch each other and to smile at each other.

Another way in which this class differed from other classes was that the staff were so obviously enjoying their work; they got on well together and knew that they had the support of the head teacher and the other school staff.

Children receiving education in their wards

Twelve children were described as receiving part-time education in their wards (see Table III, p. 53). Three of these children were visited by teachers for approximately one hour three or four times each week, when they were played with or taken for walks around the grounds. The other nine children received only very intermittent visits from teachers; for example during one month's observations these nine children were not visited once by a teacher. One of the ward teachers had issued a timetable, stating that she would be 'available' from 1.30 to 3.30 on Mondays, Wednesdays and Fridays, and from 9 to 12 on Tuesdays and Thursdays. However, the word 'available' was very broadly interpreted, and the teacher's visits to the wards depended on whether there was any work for her to do in the main school. For example, if a teacher in the main school was away because of illness, the ward teacher would have to take over the absent teacher's class and cancel her visit to the ward.

Properly applied, ward teaching could bring teachers and ward staff together, and thus be of benefit to the children. However, when it is organised haphazardly, with teachers visiting the wards only when they have nothing better to do, it is of little value. Closer appraisal is needed of what ward teaching actually means if these handicapped children are to receive the service they are entitled to.

Education of children with special needs

All 153 school-aged children had obvious physical disabilities of varying degrees. In addition, 27 children were known to be blind; others were suspected to be blind or partially sighted, but reliable figures could not be obtained because the school records were inclined to be contradictory. Nor was it known how many of the 153 children were deaf or had some degree of hearing loss.

Only two of the 153 children were receiving any special education suited to their individual needs as deaf or blind/deaf or cerebral-palsied children (Table IV). One of these two was 12-year-old Evelyn (described on pp. 104-107). She went full-time to a deaf/blind unit attached to an ordinary deaf school a few miles from the hospital. The other child was 12-year-old Hannah, who was very severely physically disabled by cerebral palsy but was believed to be of only slightly below-average intelligence. She went three days a week to a special day-school for physically handicapped children in the local town, where she was learning how to use a 'Possum' machine. Her needs as a cerebral-palsied child were met in this school because she came under the guidance of a teacher who had had many years experience with cerebral-palsied children in Spastics Society schools.

Six of the hospital schools received occasional visits from a peripatetic teacher of the deaf, but these teachers did not advise on any of the special-care ward children. When questioned about the children's possible hearing losses, the school staff in five of the eight hospitals were adamant that "these children cannot be tested because they are deaf and dumb". Anne's story is typical of what may happen to children with sight and hearing defects when they live in long-stay hospitals. She was five years old and handicapped by the effects of rubella. She had been admitted to hospital when she was three, when her mother had had an accident and was temporarily unable to look after her, but had not been discharged from hospital when her mother recovered because the consultant advised her mother that it would be better for Anne to remain permanently in hospital.

Anne had been attending full-time school in her hospital for two years, but had not received any specialist educational help for her sight and hearing losses. She did not wear a hearing-aid or glasses. The head teacher said "I see no future for her except to remain here. She cannot be tested for hearing as there are no tests for subnormal children". The ward staff said: "subnormal children cannot be tested or wear hearing-aids. She is mute, so she will never leave the hospital".

She had enough sight to be able to watch a large, white moving object, (e.g. a person moving across the room in a white coat). She would also turn her head if called and would put up her arms to be lifted. She could take a cup with both hands if it was held close to her and could feed herself with a biscuit if it was put in her hand. She could also walk on her knees if her hands were held, and could take a few walking steps upright if somebody held her hands. She made "eh-eh" noises. It seems, therefore, that she had abilities which could have been built on.

When Anne was four her hearing had been tested by a teacher from a nearby private school for the deaf, but nobody in the hospital school was sure who had asked this teacher to test her. The report of the test said ". . . although the response was not very definite, we detected a reaction on both sides to primary tests covering various frequencies. We should like to confirm this assessment in 12 months time". When Anne's teacher was asked what had resulted from this testing and if future plans had been made for Anne, she replied: "Somebody did say, months ago, she should be assessed, but nothing's happened yet". It is surprising that the teacher who had tested Anne had merely recommended that she should be retested in 12 months time, as if regarding the test as an end in itself and not as an opportunity to advise on educational help in the meantime, or to make recommendations for better placement than in a hospital where her needs were not being met.

The local education authority's senior peripatetic teacher of the deaf said that he knew nothing about Anne, because nobody had informed him about her presence in the hospital or asked for his advice about her. He did not himself check to see if any rubella children were in the hospital and needing special help, nor did the head teacher of the hospital school have any communication with the peripatetic teachers of the deaf. This case suggests that there needs to be far more contact between local education authority peripatetic teachers of the deaf and teachers of multiply handicapped children in long-stay hospitals.

Anne went to school every day in the hospital, but no programme had been devised to help her interpret her environment. She received no help in learning to dress herself or in finding her way about the classroom, nor in feeling faces, mouths and ears in order to learn about other people. The classroom staff had never had any advice about how to give her speech-training, and had no idea how much she could see. They sometimes helped her to kneel or to take a few steps, and she was sometimes tickled, but otherwise she received little attention at school. Most of the time she lay on the floor of the classroom with her face turned towards the sun shining through the windows. One afternoon she spent an hour sitting on the doorstep of the schoolroom, staring straight at the sun, her head held sideways.

TABLE IV

Special educational services (*i.e.* for deafness, blindness, cerebral palsy) being received by 153 multiply handicapped children aged between 5 and 15 years

Hospital	Educational service for deaf children	Educational service for blind children	Educational service for deaf/blind children	Educational advice for cerebral palsy
Ash	—	—	—	—
Bay	—	—	—	—
Birch	All the children in the hospital school had had audiology assessment two years earlier, but no follow-up for special-care children			—
Elm		One child had received advice from RNIB Educational Adviser	—	—
Larch	—		One child attended local deaf/blind unit for full-time education	—
Oak		Hospital had blind unit, but took no children from special-care ward	—	—
Willows	—	—	—	—
Pine				One child went to a local day-school for physically handicapped children on three days a week

68

Thirty miles away from Anne's hospital, a deaf/blind boarding unit had just been opened which had vacancies for rubella-damaged children, but Anne was not likely to get a place there because nobody was responsible for co-ordinating an educational service for her. Her future seemed to be the concern neither of the head teacher in the hospital school nor of the local education authority's peripatetic teachers of the deaf. Her situation illustrates the disturbing fact that once a child goes into long-term hospital care she is likely to be cut off from local special educational services, even though the hospital itself may offer nothing to replace those services.

As well as the hospital schools failing to co-ordinate any special educational service for the blind and/or deaf children, they also seemed to be at a loss about helping cerebral-palsied children who had special needs. The following episode shows how ignorance about how to help cerebral-palsied children may lead to unfortunate exercises which do not help these children at all.

Fourteen-year-old Arthur was cerebral-palsied, non-ambulant and speechless. His only ability was to grip, hold and throw with his right hand: his left hand was virtually useless. Arthur's teacher had a good relationship with him and was concerned about how to help him. She often wheeled him along the school corridor in his baby-buggy to fetch the cartons of milk for the other children. Half-a-dozen cartons would be tucked down the side of his buggy, and when he got back to the classroom he would grab them with his right hand and toss them onto a table. He obviously enjoyed doing this, and the teacher praised him for it. Sometimes, however, the teacher made impossible demands on Arthur because of her lack of understanding about his handicap. For example, one day she sat him in front of a table, built a tower of bricks on it, put a chocolate button on the top, and then told him that he was to knock down the bricks with his "bad hand" (the left one) and then he would get the chocolate. To ensure that Arthur used the left hand, the teacher lightly tied his usable (right) hand to the side of the buggy. She then went across the room to work with another child, calling to Arthur: "Go on, use your bad hand."

Arthur was usually a very sunny-tempered child, but he became very frustrated and upset because, with his right hand restrained, he had been made completely helpless. He banged his head on the back of the buggy in protest, then bent forward and deliberately used his head to knock down the tower of bricks. The teacher, startled by the noise of the falling bricks, turned round and half-grumbled at him for "being so cunning". He was given the chocolate button, but told that he should not have used his head. The bricks were again piled up and he was once more told that he had to use his "bad hand", and the restrained hand was checked to see that it was still securely fastened. After a few minutes Arthur again used his head to knock down the bricks, and again the teacher gently chided him.

This exercise with the bricks was well-intentioned by Arthur's teacher. She believed that he should be encouraged to use his weak hand, but the hand was so stiff because of years of non-use that it was impossible for him to use it to perform the task the teacher had set for him. The only thing he learnt from the exercise was that he got a chocolate button if he knocked down the pile of bricks with his head. It would have been better to have helped him by exercising the hand every day, trying to uncurl the fingers and placing objects in it, such as small balls and bricks.

Teachers' communication with the children

None of the special-care teachers was collecting information about how the children could communicate, and no special techniques, such as British Sign Language, word-boards, or similar aids to communication were being used in any hospital school. Only Hannah, referred to on page 66, who went three days a week to a school for physically handicapped children in the community, had any opportunity to learn how to communicate (and what she was learning in that school was not being followed up consistently in the hospital).

Some teachers recognised that the children's sounds and facial expressions often had meaning, and some had excellent rapport with the children, but they found this difficult to define and could often only describe it as "we're on the same wave-length". (See pp. 24-26 for discussion of communication systems.)

Why the hospital schools were failing children with special needs

The vast majority of these multiply handicapped children were not getting the special educational services they needed, even when they were regularly attending hospital schools. In too many cases the children were merely *contained* in their hospital schools, and it seemed that leaving their wards and going to the school merely meant that the children were exchanging one inadequate environment for another.

Some of the reasons why the children were not receiving the special educational services they needed for their particular disabilities, especially blindness, deafness and cerebral palsy, were:
(1) Teachers were uninformed about their local social services and health services, and did not understand how these might tie in with special educational services.
(2) Teachers did not know how to find their way around the statutory and voluntary services in order to get a co-ordinated service for the children with special needs; for example they did not know the procedure for getting a child like Anne out of hospital and into a special boarding school, where her needs would be better met than in the hospital.
(3) Teachers were unaware of the professional advice available through national voluntary organisations such as the Royal National Institute for the Blind and The Spastics Society.
(4) Teachers were reluctant to take responsibility in the areas of the children's care which seemed to border on their medical needs.
(5) Teachers lacked educational guidelines, *i.e. how* to teach cerebral-palsied,

70

deaf or blind children.

(6) Teachers tended to keep to their own departments and to find difficulty in developing a multi-disciplinary approach to the children's needs.

Local education authority advisers

Head teachers in the hospital schools gave the opinion that there was nothing that local education authority advisers in special education could advise about multiply handicapped children, and that the main value of advisers was in negotiating between the hospital head-teachers and the local education office regarding numbers of staff and finance for equipment.

Some of the hospital schools had occasional visits from music or physical education advisers, but these were usually concerned with the provision of musical instruments or apparatus for physical education, and not to give advice on methods of teaching handicapped children. Advisers with experience in infant or nursery-school education were not involved in the hospital schools, although, as professionals with a special interest in the development of young children, they should have been able to offer valuable advice on the play and social development of the children, and perhaps draw attention to the possible effects of the institutional environment on child development.

The rôle of local education authority advisers seemed to be ill-defined with regard to hospital schools. They might have done more to ensure that hospital-school staff were better informed about the special needs of multiply handicapped children, through in-service training and visits to other schools and centres for handicapped children. They could also have taken a much stronger lead in co-ordinating the special educational services which some of the children needed, e.g. for the deaf, blind or cerebral-palsied children.

School health services

The head teacher of Larch Hospital school had invited the doctor of the local school-health services to give the children a medical examination, as part of the service available to all children in local schools. All the parents received a letter from the head teacher to tell them that their child was going to be seen by the school doctor, and inviting them to be present. This school medical examination was independent of the hospital and was made on the hospital school premises. This link with the community child-health services could have been a means of co-ordinating the health and education services the children needed, but it was said that the doctor would have "to tread very carefully" if recommending treatment or further investigations. For example she could not recommend that any of the children in the hospital should have appointments with specialists in other hospitals for ophthalmic advice or orthopaedic treatment, nor could she recommend that the children should receive physiotherapy or speech therapy as out-patients in other hospitals, even though the children were not getting all this necessary treatment in Larch Hospital.

It appeared that, because the children in the mental handicap hospital were the medical responsibility of the consultant there, the school doctor had no power to go over his head in recommending treatment elsewhere. This meant that although the school doctor could look at the children's health, her visit was really only nominal and she had no power of follow-up. Thus, these long-stay hospital children did not have the same access to the local health services as were available for children living in the community. Ostensibly confined to hospital in order to get specialist nursing and medical care, in fact the children were not getting this care in hospital, and their being in hospital prevented them from having their needs met by the child-health services outside that hospital.

Parents' contact with hospital teachers

Larch Hospital school was the only one of the eight schools to have a parent-teacher association. The association held meetings once a term, and had film shows and discussions. All the head teachers said that there was a nucleus of parents who always came to functions, such as Open Days, sports days and fetes, but others never came near. In all the hospital schools the teachers had more contact with the parents of the day children than with those of the long-stay children, and none of the special-care class teachers had much contact with the families of the long-stay children. Even in Larch Hospital, which had the best teacher-parent contact of any of the schools, the teachers were in contact with the parents of only five of the 24 special-care ward children.

Although the teachers did not seem to think that parent-teacher associations were very helpful, they would probably be a useful means of maintaining contact with parents. Nurses had found that parent contact improved when there were ward-parent groups (see p. 10 and p. 14). Because many of the parents lived a long way off and could only visit at week-ends, perhaps the formation of a combined school/ward/parents' association might have been helpful. Such an association could hold meetings at week-ends, with teachers going into the wards for the meetings or even opening the school for it. This might be a means not only of helping parents to feel more in touch with their child's school, but also of building better relationships between school staff and ward staff.

RECOMMENDATIONS

(1) The local education authority advisers should check on why some children in hospital are excluded from school or receive only part-time education. They should also check on all children who are described as 'visited on the wards', to ascertain what this means in terms of giving a service to the children, *i.e.* how *frequently* are they visited, and for how long, and what does the teacher actually do with the children, and why does she do it.

(2) The rôle of local education authority advisers in providing services for children in hospital schools should be clearly defined. They should be accountable for co-ordinating a comprehensive special educational service for multiply handicapped children, which will meet the needs of individual children who require special help because of deafness, communication problems, blindness or physical disabilities.

(3) Head teachers in hospital schools should inform peripatetic specialist teachers about the deaf and blind children in the hospitals, and the peripatetic teachers should regularly visit the special-care classes and advise the teachers on the education of children with hearing loss and sight defects, and ensure that the teachers know how to help the children use the appropriate aids.

(4) Head teachers in hospital schools should know about the professional work of voluntary organisations for handicapped children, and should obtain their educational advice on children with special needs.

(5) Special-care teachers should have opportunities to attend in-service training courses on the needs of multiply handicapped children. Courses in the care and education of children with multiple handicaps are organised by The Spastics Society's Castle Priory College in Wallingford, Berkshire, by the Hester Adrian Research Centre at Manchester University, and by the Institute of Mental Subnormality in Kidderminster, Worcestershire. However, one of the shortcomings of any course is that tutors rarely are able to follow-up the staff when they return to their place of work, so there is a danger that the children may not receive much long-term benefit from staff having been on a course. Some staff feel that, rather than going away on a course, it would be better if 'mobile' courses were available; perhaps some sort of 'teaching bus', with tutors, demonstration films, appropriate aids and literature, which would regularly visit premises and give in-service training.

(6) Special-care teachers should know about the local health services for children and how to make use of the statutory education and health services. They should be familiar with the machinery for getting children out of hospital, *i.e.* knowing what steps to take, application to voluntary society schools, assessment.

(7) Special-care teachers should know about the work of voluntary organisations for handicapped children, and should endeavour to visit appropriate schools. Two of these are Meldreth Manor, Meldreth, Cambridgeshire (a Spastics Society ESN(S) school), where educational methods are being pioneered for multiply handicapped children; and Hawksworth Hall, Guisely, near Leeds, Yorkshire, a Spastics Society school and assessment centre.

(8) Further evaluation should be made of staggered school holidays in their present form (*i.e.* children attending school all the year round). Perhaps staggered holidays would be more helpful for the children if they took the form of teachers working in the wards during the long summer closure, or

organising some special project such as a playgroup or a two-week volunteer one-to-one service.

(9) Special-care teachers should be ensured of the support of the head teacher and other hospital-school staff, so that they do not feel isolated. This support could be as encouragement to use all the facilities of the school, to have extra use of the mini-bus, and to have a regular exchange of ideas with other members of school staff.

(10) Radical changes should be made in the present concept of education for multiply handicapped children in hospital. Their disabilities and the peculiar environment make conventional teaching inappropriate, and a case could be made for teachers working different hours (evenings, week-ends), in different places (wards and therapy rooms) and with a greater concentration on multi-disciplinary work. The children could also be greatly helped by being given opportunities for experiences in the community in order to make up for the deprivations caused by living in an institution. Regular volunteers could help here, by acting as escorts for visits to shops, railway stations, towns and perhaps private homes.

(11) Children should not spend a lot of time sitting on pots in their classrooms unless it is necessary for them to do so.

(12) Teachers should familiarise themselves with the work of ward staff, for there can be no understanding without familiarity.

(13) Ward staff should be made welcome in the schools.

(14) If teachers know about poor standards of child care in the wards, they should speak openly about it to staff in other disciplines and attempt to solve the problems. For example, teachers should support the nursing staff in requests to the Area Health Authority for an increased number of nurses.

(15) School/ward/parent associations should be formed, and actively supported by the teachers.

(16) Teachers should work closely with other disciplines in using an accepted system of communication with the multiply handicapped children, which will be used generally in the daily life of the children. They should be up-to-date with current research in systems of signing, and know about the various methods (see pp. 24-26).

(17) The Department of Education and Science should issue clearly defined guidelines for teachers working with multiply handicapped children in long-stay hospitals. The guidelines should contain practical ideas, a philosophy of educational practice for multiply handicapped children, instructions on observing children and record-keeping, advice on contact with parents and the community, advice on relationships with other staff in the hospital, and recommendations on the responsibility of hospital teachers for standards of

child care in their hospitals.

(18) Doctors working in the school health services should have more executive power for recommending treatment for children in long-stay hospitals. On their recommendations, a child should be able to attend another hospital as an out-patient if the hospital in which he is living does not provide him with the medical or paramedical treatment he needs, such as physiotherapy, speech therapy, ophthalmic advice or orthopaedic services.

CHAPTER 6

The Nurses

Introduction

This chapter looks at the position of the nurses working in the wards visited in this study. Because many of the wards appeared to be giving the children such poor care, it would be easy to criticise the nurses and to cite a few instances which showed them to be uninformed and insensitive. However, it is important to remember that: (1) the majority of ward staff I met during this study were concerned and unselfish people; (2) poor practices of child care were being caused primarily by years of bad organisation and a lack of guidelines rather than by the actions of a few individuals who were working in difficult circumstances at ward level; and (3) the wards were almost always short-staffed.

Whatever the quality of care given, the staff in the special-care wards had one thing in common: they all felt *unsupported*. To what extent this was true might be argued, but if one is to understand the problems of child care in long-stay hospitals, it is necessary to recognise that as far as the ward staff were concerned they *felt* unsupported by their senior colleagues, by other disciplines in the hospital, and by the community outside the hospital.

Hours of work

Full-time nurses worked a 40-hour week in various shifts. One system was to work for three days from 7am to 2pm, then a fourth day from 7am to 5pm followed by a day and a half off duty. Another was to work three 'long' days from 8am to 8pm (with half-hour breaks in the morning and afternoon and 45 minutes for lunch), on the fourth day to work from 8am to 5.30pm, and then have two whole days off.

Organisation of ward staff

All the wards were in the charge of a Registered Nurse for the Mentally Subnormal (RNMS). Some had two RNMS jointly in charge, each working a different shift, while others had an RNMS in charge, with a State Enrolled Nurse (SEN) as a deputy. Only one nurse had qualifications related specifically to children; this was a Sister who was a Registered Sick Children's Nurse (RSCN) and who had the certificate of the Nursery Nurse Education Board (NNEB), as well as being an RNMS.

Two-thirds of the ward staff were unqualified Nursing Assistants (NA), with varied backgrounds. Some described themselves as "just a housewife wanting a job now the kids are at school", while others came from employment in factories, domestic work, shops and offices. Some had been working for five or 10 years in hospitals, but had never had formal training because of family ties or because they felt that they would not pass the examinations. If a hospital did not have any in-service training courses, it was possible for NAs to work for many years and never attend one lecture, film or discussion group about children. Even in the hospitals which were providing in-service training for NAs, the content of the lectures tended to be directed towards medical and institutional aspects rather than towards child care. For example lectures on 'Basic First Aid', 'Epilepsy', 'Fire Precautions' and 'The Work of Other Hospital Departments' were useful in giving a broad view of the hospital and some medical aspects of mental handicap, but obviously they offered no insight into child development, the mothering needs of young children, how children need to communicate, or the value of play. Willows Hospital was the only one in which the in-service training for NAs included some reference to the needs of children: the film on the Brooklands Experiment* had been shown. However, Willows Hospital was small (only 200 patients) and did not have a nurses' training school, so there was no budget to cover the cost of in-service training. The only financial help they received with in-service training was an allocation from the Area Health Authority of approximately £30 a year to cover the cost of hiring films. The nursing officer in charge of in-service training at Willows Hospital appealed to the League of Friends if she wanted money to pay for speakers for meetings, or to buy journals and books.

Charge Nurses, Sisters and deputies worked full-time. They were permanently attached to the wards, and some had worked in their particular ward for more than five years. They usually had a small nucleus of two or three other permanent staff, but the majority of staff would be 'floaters', *i.e.* student nurses on three-month placement in the ward, pupil nurses, cadets, NAs loaned from other wards or university students working as NAs during their vacations. In some hospitals only one-quarter of the ward staff were permanent, and most of these were part-time workers. For example the permanent staff of Elm Hospital special-care ward were: one full-time RNMS, one full-time SEN, one part-time RMN (Registered Mental Nurse) and four part-time NAs. This ward accommodated 16 severely handicapped children, of whom three were known to be blind, all were incontinent, 15 were non-ambulant and 15 needed to be fed. Yet to care for these children there were only the two full-time permanent staff (the Sister and her deputy), both of whom worked different shifts, and they had to share the five permanent part-timers, who worked hours to suit their families. This meant that for most of the time the children were being cared for by floating staff, usually students and NAs loaned for a day from other wards. During a period of 29 days, no fewer than 21 different floating staff were sent to the ward, 17 of whom were unqualified (one being a

*The 'Brooklands Experiment' is the name now given to the study done by Jack Tizard, in which a group of mentally handicapped children were moved from a long-stay hospital to a small residential nursery, organised on principles of child care rather than of nursing and medical care. The children showed progress in social and intellectual abilities because of this change in their style of care. The work was reported in *Community Services for the Mentally Handicapped* (1964: Oxford University Press), and part of the work was also filmed.

16-year-old pupil nurse). The shortages of staff were so serious that the Sister or her deputy would sometimes be on duty for 12 hours with only one other, very inexperienced, member of staff. This ward also had as many as 17 different night-nurses in 28 nights. These constant changes of day staff and night staff meant that in one month the children had 38 floating, unfamiliar staff to look after them.

Part-time nurses

The majority of part-time nurses, whether floating or permanent, qualified or unqualified, were married women with families. In one hospital more than one-third of all the nursing establishment were married women working part-time.

Opinions varied about using a large number of married women as part-time nurses. Some hospitals permitted them to work hours to suit their families, from 10am until 3pm Mondays to Fridays, so that they could see their own children to and from school. However, this meant that these nurses were not in the wards when they were most needed for the handicapped children, at breakfast-time, bed-time, evenings and week-ends. Some wards had six part-time nurses on duty between 10am and 3pm from Monday to Friday, when the children were at hospital school, but in the evenings, when there were more than 20 children back in the ward needing mothering and play attention, there could be only two nurses on duty.

Advocates of part-time staff maintained that it was a form of 'recruiting insurance'; they believed that part-timers became full-timers when their children grew up. However, there was no certainty about this, and as their employment in the meantime did not substantially benefit the handicapped children who needed individual care, the theory seemed to have a dubious basis.

Duties

The nurses' duties could be divided into six main categories:

(1) *Duties requiring personal contact with the children in the course of providing physical care:* dressing/undressing; washing; changing; feeding and giving drinks; doing hair; cleaning teeth; bathing; cutting nails; toileting.

(2) *Duties requiring personal contact with the children in the course of providing 'home-nursing' care:* giving enemas; giving out drugs and medicines (generally only done by qualified staff or third-year students); attending to injuries (simple falls, bruises, cuts); caring for children who were unwell, but not ill enough to be transferred to the hospital block or a general hospital (*e.g.* a child with a non-infectious skin disease, or bronchitis, or recovering after a major fit, or convalescent after a childhood illness).

(3) *Duties requiring contact with the children in the course of providing recreation, education or medical care away from the ward:* escorting children to and from the hospital school; wheeling children around the grounds for a walk; escorting children on outings, *e.g.* to the sea; escorting children to and

from therapy; escorting children to the hospital block or to a general hospital for treatment, such as X-rays or dental care.

(4) *Domestic-type chores not requiring contact with the children:* preparing and serving food, *e.g.* liquidising, chopping; getting meal trolley ready: putting out plates, spoons; making children's drinks (cocoa, tea, orange juice); bed-making; turning down beds; bundling up dirty laundry; fetching clean laundry; sorting clean laundry and putting it away; bundling up individual children's clothes ready to wear on the following day; marking new clothes with children's names; pairing socks; pairing shoes and slippers; washing items of children's personal clothing; tidying the bathroom, lavatories, bedroom and day-room; putting clean sheets onto mattresses on the day-room floor, into armchairs and over bean-bags; wiping tables; wiping out pots; mopping floors; tidying the courtyard; tidying cupboards (linen-stores, toys); tidying children's lockers; washing wheelchairs; boiling flannels; washing dishes; fetching medicines from the pharmacy; sorting and fetching supplies (talc, soap, ointments).

(5) *Personnel work, not necessarily requiring contact with the children:* talking to parents; talking to volunteers and showing them what to do; talking to official visitors.

(6) *Work mainly done by the nurse in charge, not necessarily requiring contact with the children:* writing reports; talking to the doctor, if he visited; instructing students.

Some of the nurses' work listed above is entirely domestic (*e.g.* washing up and mopping floors) but because of shortage of domestic staff as a result of sickness or holidays, these jobs would not have got done if the nurses had not done them. It is also important to note that more than half the jobs listed did not require the nurses to be involved with the children.

Housekeepers

Two of the eight hospitals employed housekeepers. Their duties included: washing children's personal clothing and ironing, mending and marking clothes with children's names; tidying lockers; dusting; cutting bread-and-butter and making children's drinks. They did not do any messy jobs, such as washing dirty pants. The care of the children's clothes was noticeably better when wards had housekeepers. Another point in their favour was that they were permanently attached to the ward and sometimes got to know the children well. Sometimes they helped to make beds or feed children if the ward was particularly short-staffed, and sometimes they went on outings with the children. They worked from Monday to Friday, from 8am until 4.30pm or from 8.30am until 5pm.

Shortage of staff

Shortages of staff were a serious problem in the wards. The following list of staff in Larch Hospital's special-care ward shows that there were as many as

92 out of 102 day-shifts when four or less nurses were on duty*:

two nurses on duty: 2 shifts
three nurses on duty: 13 shifts
four nurses on duty: 77 shifts
five nurses on duty: 9 shifts
eight nurses on duty: 1 shift

(the last shift, when eight nurses were on duty, was on Christmas morning, when staff volunteered to do an extra duty).

Twenty-seven children lived in that ward, of whom five were blind, 24 were incontinent and non-ambulant, and 19 needed to be fed. With so few staff, the work of caring inevitably became merely a matter of moving from one routine task to another: washing, changing, feeding, with brief coffee-breaks in between. In these circumstances it was impossible to satisfy the children's mothering needs, and it was plain that the shortages of staff were causing poor patterns of child care, and also resulting in stress and physical exhaustion for the staff.

In all the hospitals, shortages of staff occurred most frequently during the evenings, first thing in the mornings and during week-ends. The following incidents illustrate what shortages at these times meant for the staff. They all occurred in Elm Hospital's special-care ward, which accommodated 16 very severely disabled children.

A Monday: a student, who had only entered the nursing school six weeks earlier, was alone on duty from 7.15am until 9.15am. She had to feed the 16 children and then begin to get them out of bed. The nursing officers knew that she was alone.

A Wednesday: one SEN was alone on duty from 7.15am until 9am. She rang the nursing office at 7.30 and said: "I've got 16 spastics on my own, I must have some help." She was told that somebody would be sent, but nobody came. By the time the two members of the regular day-staff came on duty at 9 o'clock, the SEN had finished feeding the children and was just beginning to get some of them out of bed and washed.

A Thursday: Luke, a nursing assistant, was on his own from 5pm until 6pm, when another assistant came to help him for the rest of the evening. Luke had been working in the hospital for eight weeks and had not been in the ward before. He was not introduced to the children because the student nurse and pupil nurse who had been in charge since 4pm left immediately he arrived at 5pm. He knew nothing about handicapped children, and was nervous at suddenly being in charge of so many helpless children. Before becoming a

---

*The DHSS recommendations for staffing of mental handicap hospitals are laid out in the DHSS Letter to Regional Hospital Board Chairmen (DS 10/69 and 10/70), as outlined yearly in Form SBH 12. *"Improved conditions and support for staff.* Provision of a nurse:patient ratio of not less than 1:1.4 staffed available beds, which is estimated to be the average of ratios ranging from 1:1 for very high dependency to 1:8 for 'hostel type' patients. These ratios apply to ward staff only and exclude nurses engaged on administrative, tutorial and other duties." (Special-care wards would be classified as high dependency.)

nursing assistant, Luke had been working as a clerk.

A Sunday: There was only a first-year student nurse and a new nursing assistant to look after the 16 children in the 12½ hours between 7.15am and 7.45pm. When one of these two went for lunch and tea breaks, the other was alone. During the getting-to-bed period between 5pm and 7pm, the student 'did' nine children by strip-washing them on a bed, taking approximately 13 minutes to do each child. Between 6pm and 7pm the nursing assistant bathed five children, taking approximately 12 minutes to do each child. Afterwards they had to tidy the bathroom and bundle up the laundry bags. (I bathed the last two children.)

Following are some examples of how the shortages of ward staff were affecting the care given to the children in the various hospitals.

Physical care was poor
The same bowl of water might be used for washing as many as eight children, simply because the staff were too dispirited to keep changing the water: by the time the last child was washed the water was cold and slimy.
Children often were left sitting on pots in the 'potty' room for as long as an hour or an hour and a half.
The children lacked fresh air because the staff were unable to cope with the physical effort of getting them outside when there were perhaps only three nurses to more than 25 helpless children.
The organisation of feeding was sometimes so confused that some children were likely to get two puddings and no first course, while others went without their pudding or without a drink.

A therapeutic environment was not possible
The main aim of many ward staff had become how to get through the shift and complete the basic routine duties. There was no time to think about the children who needed special consideration or methods of care because of their handicaps.

Mothering care and play was minimal
Floating staff came and went, and some never even learnt the names of the children.
Tiredness sometimes made the staff lose their tenderness for the children.
Many of the children were very lonely: for example 12-year-old Ralph, who had been in hospital for six years and was totally blind, was sat in front of the television every evening for two to three hours, and received no mothering attention during that time. (See Chapter 7 for further discussion of the children's mothering and play needs.)

Professional depression
As noted in the previous pages, shortages of staff were a cause of poor standards of child care. When there was only one nurse to care for between

seven and 10 severely handicapped children, there was no time to mother the children or help them to play or move or communicate. It is sobering to realise that there would be an outcry of public sympathy, and help would be mobilised from the local authority social services department, if a social worker found a single parent trying to look after 10 severely handicapped children on her own. Yet nurses in long-stay hospitals, who are frequently placed in this intolerable situation and may justifiably be likened to un-supported parents, do not have their plight recognised as a social problem. Instead, they are expected to cope with their problems without complaint, and without neglecting the children.

It is feasible to suggest that because the nurses were unable to fulfill their work as they knew it should be fulfilled, and because they felt unsupported in their problems, many were suffering from the same sort of depression that affects unsupported parents. In effect, they were suffering from what I term *professional depression*. This was especially obvious among qualified staff, and it poses the question of how fair it is to train nurses and then leave them unsupported in stressful situations which inevitably will destroy their professional enthusiasm. Many of the nurses I met during the course of this study had been disappointed in their aspirations about their work, but they felt unable to change the structure of an institution which was not only denying them professional fulfillment but was also encouraging poor habits of child care.

Professional depression appears to come about during the course of the following, typical situations:

(1) A nurse trains and qualifies as a Registered Nurse for the Mentally Subnormal. Intellectually stimulated by three years as a student, he has bright expectations of his career and the work he hopes to do for handicapped people.

(2) He receives a post as a deputy charge-nurse. He feels inhibited by being under a charge nurse whom he considers unimaginative, but he looks forward to having his own ward and to being 'his own boss'.

(3) Three years later he becomes the charge nurse of a ward for multiply handicapped children. The ward has a reputation for being hard, for it accommodates 20 very severely handicapped children, but he thinks of this as a challenge and looks forward to making changes in the ward.

(4) He and his deputy (a near-retiring SEN) and a part-time nursing assistant are the only regular staff in the ward. They have to rely on a series of floating unqualified staff. Only one-third of the children are accepted by the school. There are no physiotherapists or speech therapists working in the hospital, and the consultants rarely visit the ward. The psychologists tell him that his children are too dull to be helped. The occupational therapists only work with adults. Volunteers are not sent to the ward because the Voluntary Service Organiser thinks they will be 'put off' by the children's handicaps. There is a

shortage of wheelchairs and furniture, so it is impossible to give the children the outings they need or to sit them up properly to feed them. The laundry services are inefficient and the staff get irritable with each other because of linen shortages. Any ideas he tries to put into practice fail because his two permanent long-established staff are not enthusiastic about them. He tries to start a playgroup on the ward, but this folds up after six weeks. Faced with problems which he cannot solve, and working in uncongenial surroundings, the charge nurse finds that he is getting seriously overtired. He begins to feel ineffectual, and suffers from a perpetual feeling of futile anger.

(5) He finally becomes hardened to his problems. He stays in that ward as charge nurse for years, accepting his ineffectuality and giving up all attempts to make things better. He even adopts a non-caring, almost jocular, manner about the problems. New young deputies find him uninspiring to work with, and they move on as soon as possible. Students regard him as a 'stick-in-the-mud', and as an obstruction to their ideas, and they wonder why he has never bothered to change things. They resolve not to be like him when they qualify.

One of the State Enrolled Nurses I met during this study, who had been working in special-care wards for 20 years, said: "I've seen so many new young sisters and charge nurses give up. How long will it be before she (referring the the new Ward Sister) gets fed-up? She'll soon be like the rest of us. You only get a bad name if you keep fighting for things; you get labelled as a trouble-maker. So you keep quiet in the end." The new Sister had been trying to get suitable furniture for her cerebral-palsied children, but her enthusiasm was being dampened by the older, long-established staff in her ward, and her failure to get her children recognised as having special needs was making her dispirited. She said: "I begin to hate my job, knowing I shall never be able to change things. I dread coming in sometimes, yet when I trained I enjoyed my work."

Nurses are often accused of not campaigning enough to improve conditions in hospitals, but this may well be because they are often physically exhausted, and this exhaustion contributes to professional depression and makes them appear apathetic. When one nurse has to bathe nine heavy spastic children single-handed, standing for two hours in a hot, noisy bathroom, she is left sweating and tired, with aching muscles and sore feet. At the end of an evening she has too little emotional or physical energy left even to pick up a child and cuddle him, let alone campaign for better conditions.

It was rare for the staff to blame the severity of the children's handicaps for their feelings of stress. Their sense of failure was always blamed onto the organisation of the hospital which was preventing them from doing their best for the children. An RNMS, mother of three young children and working full-time in a special-care ward, said: "I feel guilty because I cannot care for these handicapped bairns as I would my own, because of all the other ward duties that we have to do—that's where the stress lies." Talking of their feelings about the children's handicaps, most special-care ward staff said that

83

they were "upset at first" but "soon got used to seeing them". A ward sister said the children had "made a terrible impact" on her when she had first seen them as a 16-year-old nursing cadet, but now she was used to them. An SEN said: "My first day I went home and cried my eyes out and said to my husband I'd not go back in the morning, but three years later I'm still here".

Although the staff denied that they were distressed by the children's handicaps, the extent to which they really were 'used to' seeing such extremely severe handicaps might be debatable. They might have found it helpful, for example, if their hospitals had had an organised policy of discussion and counselling to enable a supportive philosophy to be worked out about the place of severely handicapped children in society and the best ways in which to help them.

Being in a similar position to unsupported parents because of staff shortages and physical overwork, and lacking counselling or any secure philosophy of care for the children, it was inevitable that the staff should suffer from professional depression. It is surprising that this very real malaise, which appears to affect so many ward staff and which causes poor care to be perpetuated, has not yet been recognised by the DHSS or by planners of services for mentally handicapped people, nor by the investigators of the various long-stay hospital scandals which have occurred.

Isolation in the hospital

In some of the hospitals visited during this study, it seemed that the professional depression of special-care ward staff was being exacerbated because their wards were left out of the mainstream of developments in the hospital. It was not surprising that, like underprivileged parents, the special-care nurses cast envious eyes on expensive new projects taking place in their hospitals which were not going to benefit *their* children. They felt they were the Cinderellas of a Cinderella service, forgotten not only by the world outside the hospital but also by their colleagues in the hospital itself. For example, some special-care wards were desperately short of furniture and staff, yet thousands of pounds might be spent in developing well-furnished and well-staffed out-patient and assessment departments in the hospital. One hospital had an Assessment Unit which accommodated six children for approximately four weeks at a time, and the staff of the Unit consisted of:

    two full-time qualified nurses
    one full-time nursing assistant
    one part-time qualified nurse
    one part-time nursing assistant
    one third-year student nurse
    one night nurse
    one full-time secretary
    one full-time administrator
    one part-time clerk
    one part-time physiotherapist

84

one full-time teacher
one full-time psychologist
one part-time occupational therapist
one part-time speech therapist.

There were also seven doctors attached to this Unit, and an audiologist, a dentist and an ophthalmologist visited on a part-time basis.

The amount of professional expertise concentrated on that one Unit was regarded with bitterness by the staff of the long-stay children's special-care wards which were not visited by therapists and psychologists, and rarely even received a visit from a doctor. While one can appreciate the necessity to develop good assessment facilities and support for out-patients, surely it is also important that long-stay children receive a similar standard of professional support.

The 'Cinderella' feeling that special-care ward staff have is reinforced by the organisational philosophy of mental handicap hospitals, which advocates the *grading of patients*. This process of grading people, inherent in institutional thinking, makes it difficult to effect changes for those at the bottom. Multiply handicapped children are regarded as being the lowest grade of all, and being the last in the pecking order of the institution, they and their staff are likely to receive least resources and support. The words used in the hospitals to describe the wards for multiply handicapped children were an indication of the negative attitudes towards the children, caused by the tradition of grading patients; for example "high-dependency ward", "special-care ward", "babies' ward", 'cot-and-chair ward", "low-grade" (used mainly by long-established staff), or even "the vegetable patch" (staff slang).

Discussing the advantages of working in wards for more able children, the special-care staff agreed that the staff of the ambulant children's wards received:

(a) *more professional stimulation:* for example their children were more likely to get the help of psychologists, plans were made for the children's rehabilitation, and staff were given some professional aims to work to.

(b) *more physical relief:* for example the children were less helpless so there was less lifting and feeding to do; outings were more frequent, to interesting places — shopping or perhaps even to holiday camps. Although these activities were tiring, they offered a stimulus which was not available to the staff in special-care wards.

Job satisfaction

In view of what has been discussed in the foregoing sections about shortages of staff, professional depression, and isolation within the hospital itself, the question arises as to whether there can be *any* satisfaction for nurses working in special-care wards. Lacking guidelines on how to care for multiply handicapped children, and lacking specialist support, the special-care ward nurses appear to be merely ticking over in an endlessly repetitive performance of routine domestic tasks.

The nurses described the following as their main sources of job satisfaction:
(1) *Companionship:* "A lot of my friends work in the hospital" (NA); "I enjoy the company, it takes me out of the house" (part-time RNMS, married, with a family); "We work together, have a laugh, you have to keep cheerful and not think about the work too much" (RNMS, male, in charge of special-care ward for 10 years).
(2) *The need for money:* "I used to work in an office, but this is better money, although I don't like doing it" (NA).
(3) *Keeping the ward ship-shape:* "It's a sort of challenge to get all the work done" (full-time SEN); "I like the routines" (NA).
(4) *Liking children:* "They need you and you grow to love them" (married Sister, RNMS); "I love the kids, and wouldn't change my job for anything" (full-time SEN); "It's like looking after your own bairns again" (NA, with grown-up family, working full-time).

Although they were overworked for a greater part of their time, many staff did derive genuine satisfaction from the routine work of washing, bathing and feeding the children and keeping the ward tidy. To see the children all finished and tucked into bed, to know that one has 'pulled one's weight', to have the bathroom tidy and ready for the next morning's shift, and to have survived a rushed evening with no mishap — although there may have been only three staff for 27 children — could give an understandable sense of satisfaction. This satisfaction in completing routine tasks should not be decried: denied the ideal of having small numbers of children and being able to give individual mothering care, the nurses could often do little more than take a pride in performing the routine work as efficiently as they could. However, concentration on completion of tasks was likely to prevent the staff developing personal relationships with the children, because so many of the routine tasks were entirely domestic (*e.g.* pairing socks, sorting slippers, putting away linen, making beds) and did not require personal contact with the children. These routines would take place while the children sat without personal attention. In fact, because the organisation of the ward necessitated the regular completion of routine tasks, it was easy for the nurses to form a *habit of non-involvement* with the children, a habit which could become so deep-seated that even when the numbers of staff were increased, the children still failed to get individual mothering care because the staff were so accustomed to concentrating on routine work.

This habit of getting satisfaction from routine tasks rather than from involvement with the children was clearly stated by one of a group of nurses faced with the children all staying in the ward one day because the hospital school had a holiday. She said: "if the children weren't here it would be o.k., but we can't do our work when they are around". There were then six nurses on duty for 16 children, but their habits of non-involvement with the children had become so ingrained that they were inclined to regard the children as an interruption to their routine domestic tasks.

When student nurses enter a ward in which there is this concentration on completing routine tasks rather than on making relationships with the children, they often find themselves at loggerheads with the long-standing staff because the students' interests usually lie more with the children than with the completion of ward routines. However, many students soon get drawn into finding satisfaction in routine work. As one SEN said: "All students start off with ideals and want to help the children to walk and play, but they have to roll up their sleeves in the end and realise that they cannot waste time in playing with the kids". (See pages 92-94 for further discussion of student nurses.)

Getting ahead of routines: a characteristic habit of work

Because the organisation of all mental handicap hospitals is similar and encourages staff to concentrate on routine tasks, the special-care ward staff in the eight hospitals all had characteristic habits of work. One of these characteristics was *getting ahead of routines.* For example at about 2.30pm the children's night-clothes would be laid out ready on their cots and the bed-clothes would be turned back; 'bath bundles' would be done, *i.e.* each child who was due for a bath would have a bundle (a towel, clean nappies, pyjamas and flannel) prepared and laid on his bed or on a shelf in the bathroom. Preparation for meal-times would also be started early; at 11.20am, some 40 minutes before lunch was due to arrive, the children in some wards were put in their places to wait for it, children in wheelchairs being placed in a row and the more able children being sat at tables. The food-serving trolley would be put into the corner of the room, stacked with spoons, plastic dishes, jug of water, a pile of bibs, and a plastic bowl to receive waste slops; the staff would then stand by the serving hatch of the day-room until the meal arrived from the central kitchen. In one hospital the staff seemed to regard it as a point of honour to get as many children as possible 'done' (into night-clothes) before supper at 5pm, and if they managed to do 10 children they considered they had done well.

The almost ceremonial manner in which the staff of some wards made these early preparations for bed-times, bath-times, and meal-times gave a structure to the work, but hardly enhanced the standards of child care. Indeed, it appeared that the children had become mere appendages to a policy of saving time. A poignant example of this urge to get ahead of routines was seen in one hospital on Christmas Eve: after the children had been put to bed, some of their Christmas presents were opened by the staff and put away in order to save time on Christmas Day.

An understandable reason for the nurses developing habits of wanting to save time was that, experiencing chronic staff shortages over many years, they felt it was essential to be one step ahead in order to allow for unexpected contingencies. However, even when there were more staff, the nurses were still inclined to maintain these habits and not to involve themselves with the children.

Some recurrent tensions of work

Nurses were likely to be caused considerable tension by the following problems, which seemed to have become a standard way of life in under-staffed special-care wards.

Getting the children to school on time

The nurses' anxieties about getting children to school were likely to be increased by their poor relationships with the teachers (see pp. 56-57). Sometimes the teachers came to the ward to find out why the children had not arrived in school, and they found it looking disorganised, with food bowls lying about and dirty bed-linen. It was usual then for the teachers to go away again instead of helping, and to leave a message to "phone us when they are ready". The embarrassed nurses were left feeling like the parents of a very large and dirty family being visited by censorious school-teachers.

Not knowing how many staff would be on duty

In many of the wards there was tension first thing in the morning because, although the ward might have been allocated four staff, it was unlikely that this promise would be kept. Even if it was, during the first hour of work the staff would be on tenterhooks, expecting a telephone message from the nursing office to say that because of shortages of staff on *other* wards one of their nurses would be taken and they would have to make do with only three for the rest of the day. This reallocation occurred most frequently at week-ends. These insecure circumstances make it understandable to a degree that so many staff developed habits of getting ahead of their routine tasks instead of playing with the children.

Problems with laundry

The vexed problem of inefficient laundry services runs through the whole National Health Service and causes tension to staff at all levels. All the hospitals visited during this study had occasional shortages of towels, nappies bibs and bed-linen; and children's clothes would be lost or ruined in the wash. Shortages grew worse at week-ends and Bank Holidays, and ward staff got irritable with each other when they could not find enough nappies or towels to use. Sometimes the ward sisters resorted to hiding little caches of spare linen in anticipation of the laundry services breaking down altogether.

The 'crisis' of feeding

The children's meal-times may be described as the 'crisis' of feeding because tension tended to build up around meal-times. One reason was that if the food arrived late from the central kitchen, feeding the children overlapped with the time that nurses had to go for their own meal, and this could mean that perhaps only two nurses would be left to feed 20 or more children. At breakfast-times and lunch-times the nurses also worried about whether the meal would be completed by the time the children were to be picked up for school.

The mood in which the food was received from the central kitchen revealed the degree of staff tension at this time: the covers of the dishes were lifted and the staff invariably grumbled about the sight, smell, colour, texture and monotony of the food.

Some of the children were incredibly difficult to feed, and had to be fed on mashed food or have their food liquidised. Nurses worried about the difficulties of feeding these children and wondered whether they were getting enough nourishment. Meal-time tension was often increased because inexperienced temporary staff were on duty and they were inept at feeding difficult children. Some nurses managed to feed five or six children in an hour, others managed only two, but this slower pace did not necessarily denote better care. Sometimes there was rivalry between staff about who was most skilled at feeding certain children; and sometimes the staff would argue amongst themselves as to the best way to manage a difficult child and whether the 'food-fads' of certain favourite children should be given in to.

In some hospitals the feeding was better organised than in others. In Birch Hospital, for example, 21 children in wheelchairs were set in a large circle around the sides of the day-room, a small group of six children were sat at a table in the centre, and two children were positioned on bean-bags at the end of the room. Each child was covered in a clean draw-sheet when he was fed. The nurse would sit on a high stool beside the child to give him his two courses and his drink, then would take off his draw-sheet, wipe his face, put the dirty sheet into a laundry bag and move on to the next child. But in other hospitals the children were fed as they lay on the floor or sat slumped in armchairs, or even as they crawled about the room. Sometimes one dirty bib was used for seven or eight children. If there was a system of mass-feeding (common in several hospitals), it was possible for each child to be handled by four different nurses during one meal-time; i.e. one would put on his bib, another would feed him his meat course, a third would give him the sweet course and a fourth give him his drink and remove his bib. And if a child was being fed on the floor and crawled about between these courses, he was likely to receive his three courses in three different places in the room and with a lengthy space of time between each course. For example, one day five-year-old Anne was lifted into an armchair and a nurse fed her her meat course at 11.40; she was then put down on the floor and crawled away again until another nurse picked her up and sat her on a kitchen-type chair to feed her her pudding at 12.15. The second nurse put her down on the floor again, and a third nurse gave her her drink at 12.40 as she crawled behind a curtain. This was a typical meal-time situation for Anne. She was blind, and must have found it all very confusing, but the nurses, absorbed in their own tensions, appeared to be unaware of the effect the disorganisation might have on her. Their main aim was to get the meal finished.

In some of the hospitals, visitors were shown around the wards during meal-times, perhaps prospective volunteers, groups from women's clubs, or senior pupils from local schools. Nurses always resented this intrusion; caught at a disadvantage and stared at as they tried unsuccessfully to persuade children to swallow their food, they felt that they and the children were exposed and vulnerable. It seemed peculiarly insensitive of senior hospital staff to allow visitors into the wards at meal-times, when both staff and children were at their most defenceless.

Nurses' attitudes towards the children

Faced on the one hand by shortages of staff which prevented the development of close relationships with the children, and on the other hand by the hospital grading process which regarded multiply handicapped children as the lowest grade of all, it was not surprising that some nurses regarded the children as a group who merely required keeping warm, clean and fed. "I'm a realistic man. I have no sentimental ideas about the children; we keep them clean, feed them, given them medication, that's all we can do for them." (RNMS, 10 years in charge of a special-care ward.) "There's nothing we can do for them except keep them warm, clean and fed." (RNMS, sister for two years in a special-care ward.) The quality of the children's lives was affected to a great degree by nurses' low expectations: not expecting the children to play, they did not give them the opportunity to do so; not expecting them to learn to speak, they often failed to speak to them; not expecting them to learn to feed themselves, they often did not try to teach them to do so. While it was understandable that many nurses did have very low expectations of the children, because it *is* hard to maintain enthusiasm when faced with many children who cannot speak or walk or use their hands, it does seem imperative that staff of special-care wards should be given definite supportive guidelines instead of being left so much on their own and apparently forgotten by their nursing officers and other professionals in the hospital.

Older, long-established staff tended to have lower expectations of the children than did the newer and younger staff, partly because new staff sometimes had unrealistic expectations because of their lack of knowledge, and partly because long-established staff had developed progressively lower expectations over the years. Professional depression (see pp. 81-84) was also linked to the nurses' low expectations of the children.

Many of the nurses had an undemanding, protective attitude towards the children. A qualified nurse summed up this attitude in her words: "we accept them all in here, we do not see their handicaps, they're just children and we love and accept them". This completely uncritical acceptance was one of the finest attitudes to be found amongst special-care ward nurses. It was rarely found in other departments of the hospitals, in the hospital schools or in the community, for these less-tolerant places had definite goals to work towards and so perhaps were critical and rejecting of multiply handicapped children. However, although it was an admirable trait to be uncritical of the children, total acceptance was likely to imply low expectations. Since the only way out of the special-care ward was for a child to improve, the nurses' low expectations led them to believe that this was not possible; they made no demands on the children, for they had no goals for them.

Asked what their aims *were* for the children, some nurses said "to make them fit well into the adult wards when they grow up, without being a nuisance". This statement not only reflected the nurses' limited expectations, it also reflected lack of time they had to spare for children who *might* be a 'nuisance'. The most immediate and common expectations for a child in a special-care ward were that he should: (*a*) keep fairly still in his wheelchair so that he did not get into awkward positions which would necessitate him having to be repeatedly reseated; (*b*) keep fairly quiet (not shout, giggle or scream); (*c*) eat quickly and not spit his food back; (*d*) not smell too badly; and (*e*) sleep well at night.

Nurses' relationships and contact with other disciplines in the hospital

During our conversations, the nurses often revealed a feeling of resentment that other professionals in the hospitals did not help them more: for example, "doctors don't help us, nobody is interested in our children, nobody comes near". Other disciplines did not come forward with supportive ideas, and often the nurses themselves were too dispirited to seek help on their own initiative. Reference has already been made in Chapter 5 to the poor relationships that existed between many teachers and nurses. The nurses' relationships with other members of hospital staff were also likely to be poor.

Doctors. Nurses had very little supportive contact with doctors. They were quite pleased to see a doctor come to the ward, and they liked it if he remembered the names of staff and children. They described doctors variously, as "kind", "ordinary, although he's a doctor", or as "stuck-up" and "snobby", but they *never* described them as being good at knowing what to do about a certain child's problems. Most commonly they were described as being "out-of-touch", and their visits to the ward were regarded as a formality (*e.g.* "everything's all right, isn't it, Sister?"). (See also pp. 28-30.)

Social workers. Nurses were only likely to have had contact with social workers when a child came into the ward for a period of short-term care, when the social worker would have visited the ward to discuss the child's family background. Social workers gave no guidance on the care of the long-stay children. (See also pp. 30-32.)

Speech therapists. None of the 223 children were receiving speech therapy (see pp. 23-24). The special-care nurses who had had occasional contact with speech therapists said they found them "difficult to get on with", but perhaps this reflected the nurses' resentment of their seeming to interfere in the children's feeding methods, without understanding the problems of under-staffed wards. Again, this resentment could also have been exacerbated by the nurses' feelings of tension at meal-times.

Physiotherapists. In two of the eight hospitals the physiotherapists worked in the wards, and in doing so achieved good relationships with the nurses (see pp. 21-22). The physiotherapists' advice was not always followed by the nurses, but while they were actually in the ward the therapists could momentarily enthuse the nurses, and they were valued for any advice they could give on furniture and aids.

Occupational therapists. There was no supportive contact (see p. 26).

Psychologists. In only one of the wards did the nurses have close contact with psychologists. In this ward the psychologists had devised feeding and toilet-training programmes for a small group of specially selected, more able children. However, although the nurses appeared to get on well with the psychologists when they visited the ward to discuss the programmes, they really felt unable to carry out the programmes effectively. For example, the toilet-training programme required the installation of a system of batteries and lights in the lavatories, so that a light went on and a buzz sounded when a child urinated into the lavatory pan: the staff were then to instantly reward the child with ice-cream. However, this reward system was impossible because there were usually eight to 10 children in the lavatory area with only one nurse, and for a child to get a reward the nurse had to leave the children and go down a corridor and through two rooms to the kitchen and back again with the spoonful of ice-cream. So the batteries were turned off and the programme was discontinued, although the experiment had been set up with great enthusiasm. However, despite the fact that the batteries and lights were no longer being used, they were still shown to visitors, and the programme was explained as if it were still running. The nurses and the psychologists seemed to have a tacit agreement that, although the programme had long ceased to be a viable proposition, none of them should admit this or openly face the problems that had made it a failure, *i.e.* ward organisation and lack of staff. (For further discussion about psychologists, see pp. 26-27.)

Student nurses and the special-care wards

Seven of the eight hospitals had nurses' training schools. Although student nurses were not supposed to supplement staff shortages, they were often relied upon to look after a ward (see pp. 80-81). Some student nurses were worried because they felt that they were being given responsibility before they were ready for it. For example, one first-year student said that after only five months in the nursing school and seven weeks in the special-care ward, she was often left alone in the ward for an hour and a half.

When asked if they had complained about being left in charge of a ward, the students said that this would be difficult: one said "We are supposed to ring up the office if we are left entirely on our own in a ward, but we never do because it means filling in a form. And if a student starts complaining, then word gets around to the nursing officers and you get a bad name". Student nurses frequently felt angry at how they thought they were being exploited during their training. Many were physically tired and emotionally over-wrought, but this was not recognised by regular ward-staff, some of whom appeared to be very insensitive towards students. In one hospital it was common for students to do their first three months ward placement in a special-care ward (either adults or children), and it was said by the senior nurses that starting off students in one of the "worst wards" sorted out the weak students and "made or broke" them. A young Indian student said that, a few months after her arrival in England to start her training, she had been placed in the children's special-care ward. At that time she had had no idea that such handicapped human-beings existed, and the impact of seeing such children, on top of her homesickness, had been devastating. She said that she had wept for weeks, but had had nobody to talk to about her troubles. Such an experience suggests that long-established staff should pay more attention to the more tender feelings of some students, especially those from overseas who may already be saddened by homesickness.

Shortages of staff did not give students time to learn about the children as individuals, and the students were frustrated because what they were taught in classes could not be implemented when they got into the wards: "In lectures we are told that children need individual attention, and we know that they need more cuddling and play, but we never get time" (second-year male student). "We should let them walk to the table if they can, but they need help to walk, and they do it so slowly, it is quicker to carry them" (first-year woman student). "We've got four or five children in our ward who could maybe learn to feed themselves, but we have not got the time to teach them. It is quicker to feed them ourselves than to try and teach them" (third-year woman student).

Regarding the help given to them by their tutors, students said: "The tutors come and teach us in the wards, but we never actually talk about individual children's needs" (second-year woman student); "I'd like to know more about how to help special-care children, but we don't talk about the children as individuals" (third-year male student).

Although the students had lectures on 'teaching independence', they were rarely given any practical ideas about how to help individual multiply handicapped children to perhaps achieve such skills as how to put their arms into their cardigans or how to hold their cups. In one hospital a student had decided that she would teach 10-year-old Dick, who was partially sighted and spastic and had been in hospital for eight years, how to hold a cup. Nobody was showing her how to do this. Every day she tried to curl Dick's fingers around the cup and get him to grip it and lift it up. After several weeks her efforts resulted in Dick actually holding the cup for three minutes and trying to lift it to his mouth. The student was regarded with friendly amusement by the older staff, and described as "a typical keen young thing". There seemed to be no senior nurse, tutor or therapist, to whom she could go for advice about how to help Dick. It would appear that many students are not being well instructed about how to help multiply handicapped children, and their keenness is likely to wane through lack of encouragement in the ward and from their tutors.

The students in some hospitals said that they planned to get jobs in the community as soon as possible after they had qualified. They felt discouraged by the old-fasioned ideas of long-established staff, and believed that if they stayed working in hospitals they would get as stale as the other ward staff.

93

and instead of changing the institutions they would themselves become changed and learn to accept the old ideas.

Night nurses and special-care wards

In four of the eight hospitals there were two night-nurses on duty each night in the special-care wards, and in the other four hospitals there was only one. In some of the wards the night staff were part-timers who only worked in the hospital for two nights a week, and they were not attached to any one particular ward. This could mean that the children had very frequent changes of night staff and that some of the nurses did not know the children's names.

One ward in which only one night-nurse was on duty had 17 different night-nurses in 28 nights (see p. 78). The length of time that these particular nurses had been employed in the hospital varied from five weeks to 11 years: the one who had been working in the hospital for 11 years had qualified as an SEN through long service; the others were unqualified. Some had never been to the special-care ward before, and some had been there previously but only for one night a few months earlier or as long as a year ago. They showed little worry about being left alone in charge of children about whom they knew virtually nothing. One woman in her fifties had been working in the hospital for three nights a week for five years, to supplement her income from a fish-and-chip shop she ran in a nearby town. She usually worked in the men's wards, and had been to the children's special-care ward only once before, a year ago. She said: "I don't care where I go, one ward is the same as another as far as I am concerned".

It might be thought that it did not matter if night staff were irregular, because the children were in bed for most of the hours they were on duty. But the advantages of night staff being permanently attached to the children's wards were that if a child woke up in the night he would be reassured by having a familiar person caring for him, and it was better to be wakened in the morning by a familiar person.

Larch Hospital special-care ward had six regular night-nurses, who worked in pairs. They had all spent more than a year in the ward, some as long as five years. Three of them were qualified, (RNMS or SEN), and all six knew the children well and could describe their sleeping habits, which way they like to lie in bed, whether they were inclined to nightmares, and how they behaved first thing in the morning.

In some of the hospitals there seemed to be a lack of communication between day staff and night staff as to the part that night-nurses could take in the children's development. For example, eight-year-old Joan had been living in Pine Hospital since she was two years old; she had a very twisted spine and some speech defects but could walk and feed herself, and had good hand ability. However, when she was got up in the morning the night-nurses did not encourage her to dress herself: the senior of the two night-nurses, who had been working on the ward for a month and was an RNMS, said: "I don't know if Joan can dress herself because nobody's told me. I would make her do it if she could, but I've been told nothing". As a nurse trained to work with mentally handicapped people she should perhaps have discovered Joan's abilities herself, and encouraged her to dress herself; however, lacking initiative, she was waiting to be told what to do and did nothing because the information had not been given by the day staff.

In some of the hospitals there was ill-feeling between day staff and night staff about how much their duties overlapped, *e.g.* whether night staff should wash the children in the mornings, how much laundry sorting they should do, how many children should be left up at night for the night staff to put to bed, and whether night staff should change dirty sheets after 6.30am or leave them for the day staff to do. Generally the night staff expected everything to be ship-shape and the majority of the children to be in bed when they came on duty. It was understandable for them to expect the children to be in bed, because to be left alone to lift perhaps 20 physically handicapped children into bed could be dangerous and exhausting. But it did not seem to be entirely reasonable for the night staff to expect the day-room to be tidy when they came on duty. When asked about developing play activities in the two to three hours between supper and going to bed (approximately 5.30 to 8.30), the day staff explained that this was difficult for them to do, partly because of shortages of staff, but also because the night staff would not be pleased if they had to tidy up after the day nurses had left. This meant that during the evenings the day staff concentrated on domestic work rather than on anything which could cause a muddle, such as play activities. Therefore, between the hours of 5.30 and 8.30 the children were put into night-clothes and sat around the television set, and many sat there for the whole three hours. Some were blind children.

During the evening period, from approximately 5.30 until 8.30 or 9pm, the day nurses would first wash or bathe and change the children, and would then do the laundry, tidy the bathroom, clean the day-room, change the sheets on the mattresses in the day-room, bundle up the clothes the children would be wearing in the morning and put these ready in their lockers, make the children a drink, and write the report. Finally, they would make themselves a cup of coffee. Some of the least able of the children would perhaps be put to bed at 6 or 6.30, but the more able ones would remain up until 8.30 or 9pm, when the ward was handed over to the night-nurses. The children would receive little or no attention for several hours, apart from being given their evening drink.

In two of the hospitals a nursing assistant had been specially appointed for evening work, ostensibly to 'develop evening activities for the children'. One worked from 6 until 9pm, and the other from 6 until 10pm. However, instead of developing activities for the children, these extra members of day staff helped to get the children into night-clothes and seated in front of the television and then they, too, joined the other day staff in tidying up the bathroom, seeing to the laundry and tidying the day-room.

It would seem that, rather than spending the evening in tidying up the ward in preparation for handing over to the night staff, it might have been better for the day staff to have concentrated on giving the children some play and mothering after they had been put into pyjamas, and to have left the tidying up and laundry sorting for the night-nurses to do during the night. However, the night-nurses did not see their rôle as tidying up day-time muddles, and thus prevented the children from having possible play and mothering during the evenings.

Nurse practitioners versus nurse managers

Unit officers and the special-care wards

One of the innovations of the Salmon reorganisation of nursing (1966)[14] was that sisters and charge nurses could be promoted to the management of a small group of wards (a unit) and be known as Unit Officers. It was thought that this would not only give management opportunities and a better career structure to qualified nurses, but would also benefit the ward nurses by putting them under the direct management of somebody who was still close to problems at ward level. The unit officers would act as spokesmen for the ward nurses in matters of higher management, and give guidance at ward level as well. Ideally, unit officers would also act as spokesmen for the children in respect of management decisions.

This would seem to be the answer to the ward nurses' need for support and for a spokesman, and one could envisage the unit officers giving leadership for change, according to the needs of the ward. However, the unit officers responsible for the special-care wards did not appear to be fulfilling this rôle. Some had lost touch with the ward problems with which they had once been so familiar, and were strongly criticised by the ward nurses for shutting themselves in their offices and only coming out in order to attend meetings. They appeared to be absorbed in sorting out numbers of staff, standing in for more senior staff, showing official visitors around, and attending meetings.

In many cases there was a need for unit officers to give more effective leadership, especially in matters relating to the care of the children. For example, they should give guidelines on play, mothering, outings and child development, and should help to promote more positive relationships between ward nurses and teachers, therapists and parents. Perhaps one reason for unit officers being rather ineffective as leaders was that, after years of working in understaffed wards without any support themselves, they had come to accept the situation as inevitable and lacked ideas about how to change it.

Senior nursing officers

Another innovation of the Salmon reorganisation of nursing was that matrons and deputy matrons were replaced by principal and senior nursing-officers. These senior nurses rely on their unit officers to relay information to

14. Salmon Report (1966) *Report of the Committee on Senior Nursing Staff Structure.* (Chairman: Brian Salmon.) London: H.M.S.O.

them, and they do not have close personal contact with the wards. Many of the special-care ward nurses felt no confidence that the senior nurses understood their ward-level problems; they complained, as they did about unit officers, that senior nurses did not visit the wards unless it was to bring official visitors around.

Ward nurses had little sympathy for the management problems of senior nurses: for example those concerned with allocations of staff, interviewing staff, and acting on behalf of the hospital in negotiations with the District or the Area Health Authority. Many worries, the senior nurses said, had been caused by the 1974 reorganisation of the National Health Service. In their opinion the reorganisation had lowered morale in mental handicap hospitals because the staff felt that the management of their hospital had been taken away from them and put under people at District and Area level, who knew little about mental handicap hospitals. The principal nursing-officer in one hospital said that the reorganisation of the NHS was "a disaster" so far as mental handicap hospitals were concerned, in that it had made them more of a 'Cinderella' than ever. The members of the Area Health Authority responsible for his hospital had only visited it twice in the two years since reorganisation, and these visits were merely to have lunch and attend a meeting, not to visit the wards and learn about the problems of staff and patients.

The senior nurses in all the hospitals agreed that the now-disbanded hospital management committees had not always been dynamic, and had often consisted of too many elderly local citizens who had a benign rather than a managerial interest in the hospitals. However, looking back to the old days of hospital management committees, the senior nurses remembered them as halycon compared to the present management under the newly formed Area Health Authorities. They believed that, since 1974, mental handicap hospitals were being managed by people whose main interest lay in developing services for acutely ill people and who had little knowledge about long-stay hospitals and chronic handicaps.

RECOMMENDATIONS

(1) Nurses in long-stay special-care wards should receive the same consideration and professional support that is now being sought for parents of handicapped children.

(2) The nurses and children in long-stay special-care wards should not be excluded from the expert advice available in various new projects which their hospitals may be setting up for out-patients.

(3) Discussions should be held at ward level about the nurses' satisfaction in their work, and a regular appraisal of aims and work habits should take place.

(4) Area Health Authorities should consider an increase in the number of ward staff to be a priority in their budget plans.

(5) Floating staff should be kept to a minimum in children's wards.

(6) The employment of part-time nurses, at hours which suit their families but not the handicapped children, should be discouraged.

(7) Housekeepers should be employed in all children's wards.

(8) Visitors to the wards should not be shown around at meal-times; nor at any other time without explicit permission, in advance, from the ward.

(9) All hospital laundry services should receive attention, perhaps being examined at DHSS level.

(10) Special-care ward nurses should have opportunities to visit local centres for multiply handicapped children, for regular meetings and advisory discussions.

(11) Special-care ward nurses should receive more support from therapists, doctors, psychologists, social workers, teachers and volunteers, especially in the development of more active methods of caring for the children. For example, various methods of communication and movement and play should be explored as a multi-disciplinary study; and therapists and teachers should be practically involved in the wards.

(12) Student nurses should be given more support if they wish to develop their ideas of better child care in the long-stay wards. Tutors and ward nurses should encourage students to take an interest in individual children and in child development. Students should not be required to supplement staff shortages.

(13) There should be continuity of night staff in children's wards.

(14) Night staff should be aware of the children's abilities and individual needs; they should take more responsibility for teaching the children independence.

(15) Night staff should accept a wider range of duties, for example, bagging up day-time laundry and tidying up the day-room after play activities: this would allow the day staff to develop some evening activities for the children.

(16) Unit officers should be accountable for the development of play activities, standards of child care, and the counselling of nurses working with multiply handicapped children.

(17) Senior nursing officers should make certain that the nurses in long-stay special-care wards do not feel forgotten.

(18) In-service training for nursing assistants should include lectures and practical demonstrations about child development, play, and the mothering needs of young handicapped children in institutions.

(19) Area Health Authority members should take a more active interest in the

ward-level problems facing nurses caring for multiply handicapped children in mental handicap hospitals.

(20) Wiser use should be made of nurses' interests in individual children: for example, if a nursing assistant is particularly interested in helping one child to achieve some ability, such as holding a cup or crawling, this should be encouraged. She should have opportunities to seek advice from therapists or psychologists, or at handicapped children's centres outside the hospital.

(21) The numbers of children should be reduced in special-care wards. All nurses agreed that to have more than 12 multiply handicapped children looked after by only two to four nurses was an impossible situation; and having more than 20 in the ward was not only causing the children to suffer from emotional deprivation but could be physically dangerous as well, in that a child could fall, choke, or injure himself and perhaps be unnoticed. Ideally, at all times of the day (except when staff are taking a short break), there should never be more than eight children to five staff. (The premises visited for this study in which the staff were giving the children most attention had a ratio of seven to nine staff for nine children. See p. 104.)

(22) Guidelines should be discussed and drawn up by nurses at all levels, and other disciplines, to give clear, practical standards for the care of multiply handicapped children in institutions, and the aims and philosophy of care. All nurses at ward level should be familiar with these guidelines. They should contain references to the child-oriented matters which feature in this report, such as the need to speak to and touch the children; beneficial ways of grouping the children; and the assignation of particular staff to particular children. The recommendations in the following chapter on mothering and play would form a basis for such guidelines.

CHAPTER 7

Mothering and Play

Introduction

The quality of a child's life when he is in residential care is in large part determined by the extent to which his needs for mothering* and play are met. Given adequate mothering and play opportunities, a child may be helped to find a happy, confident place in his environment, although separated from his family. Mothering and play are inseparable. In its broadest sense, the mothering of young children in residential care covers the opportunities they are given to form a loving, reliable attachment to one or two particular members of staff and close relationships with others; and play in its broadest sense means the children having adequate opportunities to explore their environment, experiment with what they find, and learn about themselves and other people as they do so.

Because very severely multiply handicapped children have their lives complicated by gross physical, sensory and mental disabilities, it is very difficult for them to seek mothering or to initiate play. For this reason it is important that the residential care of young multiply handicapped children should be planned so as to give full consideration to these needs. Staff should be fully aware that, in order to meet them adequately, they will have to deliberately extend themselves towards the child and not wait for the child to make the first approach. Staff should also be aware that if they do *not* extend themselves to children who are too incapacitated to seek mothering or to play on their own, the children will be very lonely, and may become quiet and withdrawn; they may not make eye-contact, they may stop stretching out their hands, they may cease to vocalise, and some may develop bizarre, self-absorbing patterns of behaviour.

This chapter discusses the mothering and play needs of the 223 children in this study.

Records of attention given to the children

Ward observations showed that the children were receiving an average of approximately one hour of *physical-care attention* (washing, dressing, feeding, changing) and five minutes of *mothering attention* (cuddling, play and talking to) in a 10-hour period. A few children received more than this average, but many received far less. For example, in one ward accommodating 24 children aged from five to 21, observations made over one week-end (11 hours on Saturday and eight hours on Sunday) recorded that the children received between them a total of 30 minutes mothering in 19 hours, or 1 minute 15

*See footnote on p. 6 for definition of 'mothering'.

100

seconds each.

Table V gives examples of the amounts of attention given to 22 of the children in four of the hospitals.

What the children did

Many of the children spent hours lying on bean-bags, or sitting in wheelchairs or small armchairs, and they were only moved or touched when they needed some routine physical care. One day, during a school holiday, 11-year-old Florence, who was non-ambulant and speechless and had been in hospital for seven years, spent from 9.50am to 6.30pm sitting in her wheelchair. She was lifted out only once, to have her nappy changed after lunch (this took five minutes). Thus she spent 8 hours and 35 minutes in her wheelchair without any change of position. The chair stood in the same place all the time. She had no toys, and only received attention when she was being fed and changed. This was a typical day for Florence, and for many of the other children in the study.

Fifteen-year-old Bob had been in hospital for nine years: he was non-ambulant and speechless. The following record of one day is typical of the sort of life he led during week-ends and school holidays.

7.15am: Bob was lying awake in bed.

9.35: still in bed, he was fed his breakfast. This took 10 minutes.

10.15: he was taken out of his bed, laid on another bed, washed and dressed. This took 15 minutes.

10.30: he was placed in an armchair in the day-room.

11.55: he was lifted from the armchair and put up to the table to wait for his lunch.

12.40pm: he was fed his lunch. This took eight minutes. He remained sitting at the table afterwards.

2.15: he was lifted down from the table and had his nappy changed. This took five minutes. He was then put back into a small armchair in the day-room.

3.55: Bob was lifted up to the table to wait for his supper.

4.30: he was fed his supper: this took five minutes. He remained sitting at the table afterwards.

5.50: he was taken to be bathed and put into pyjamas. This took 15 minutes.

6.05: he was back in the day-room, being put into an armchair again. The chair was dragged into the middle of the room to be nearer the television set.

7.35: he was given a warm drink.

8.15: he was put to bed.

Bob's whole day had been spent in waiting for the next routine to be done to him. He had not received any mothering or play attention from the time he woke up until the time he went to bed. He had sucked his hands most of the time.

Play habits

The dearth of personal attention and the hours of loneliness appeared to

TABLE V

Examples of amounts of attention given to 22 children in four hospitals

Child	Age (yrs)	Years in hospital	Period of continuous day-time observation (hrs:mins)	Amount of time given to: Routine physical care* (mins)	Amount of time given to: Mothering† (mins)	Total amount of attention given during observation period (mins)
Charlotte	2	1	10:20	43	21	64
Vernon	3	1	10:20	54	—	54
Milly	4	2	10:20	41	15	56
Paul	10	½	13:00	65	10	75
Godfrey	10	8	10:05	57	—	57
Martin	10	4	13:00	68	—	68
Jack	11	10	10:20	41	21	62
Daphne	11	4	9:50	67	—	67
Florence	11	7	6:30	25	5	30
Walter	12	8	9:05	36	3	39
Norman	12	4	10:10	57	—	57
Lewis	13	10	10:20	43	—	43
Katherine	13	6	6:15	28	—	28
Vera	13	13	4:55	19	—	19
Helen	13	6	5:25	13	—	13
Gilbert	14	14	10:20	43	—	43
Jerry	14	6	7:10	30	—	30
Malcolm	17	6	7:00	23	—	23
George	17	13	10:20	49	3	52
Peggy	18	13	7:00	21	—	21
Iris	19	11	10:20	41	2	43
Stanley	20	12	10:20	41	6	47

*Washing, feeding, bathing, dressing.
†Cuddling, play and talking to.

be the cause of some children developing odd habits of occupying themselves. 14-year-old Sally (11 years in hospital) had a habit of chewing the straps of her wheelchair. One June afternoon she spent from noon until 4pm and from 5.30pm until 8.20pm sitting in her wheelchair and chewing the end of the strap that secured her. Nobody spoke to her or touched her during that time.

The children's habits included the following:

(1) Scratching their finger-nails on the surfaces of the walls, their chairs, or the floor. This produced an interesting noise and sensory effect.

(2) Dribbling on to their hands and then rubbing them together. This appeared to give a satisfying tactile experience.

(3) Clapping saliva-covered hands together.

(4) Sucking hands.

(5) Rubbing fingers backwards and forwards in a puddle of their own saliva, tears, nose discharge, urine or vomit, on the floor or table in front of them.

(6) Pulling and shaking chairs and rattling them back and forth.

(7) Spinning the wheels of overturned wheelchairs.

(8) Sucking and/or chewing clothes, especially cuffs and collars.

(9) Banging cupboard doors or day-room doors.

(10) Making monotonous singing noises.

(11) Waving socks or shoe-laces about.

(12) Pushing or pulling shoes along on the floor.

(13) Tearing up paper.

(14) Lying on the floor and kicking at the curtains, or standing by the curtains and swinging them, or winding themselves up in the curtains.

(15) Hitting or poking at own ears, eyes, nose, mouth or head.

All these habits might be described as the typical behaviour of severely mentally handicapped children. However, it should be remembered that these children were not only mentally handicapped, but that they were also severely deprived of mothering and play activities, and it is possible that their peculiar and perseverative behaviour was being aggravated by this deprivation. Seeking occupation from their limited environment, such as playing with the straps of wheelchairs, or with their own saliva, was a means of filling the time.

It was noticeable that there were some differences in the children's habits, according to their physical ability. The more mobile children tended to shove at chairs and slam doors, while the immobile children, who were all the time anchored in armchairs, bean-bags or wheelchairs, tended to suck their hands, chew their clothes and suck straps. It would seem that the children's behaviour develops from what is immediately available in their environment, *i.e.* what they are able to reach. It was also possible that the children copied each other's habits, and that stereotyped habits were being passed on from one generation of children to another. For example, 10-year-old Paul had been living in a special-care ward for six months. He was non-ambulant and speechless. He had come from a children's Home, where he had been since babyhood. There were 15 other very disabled children in Paul's ward, and they had all been living in hospital for between three and 14 years. Every day, Paul and five other children would sit in a row of armchairs, constantly chewing the front of their jumpers, their shirt-collars and their cuffs. The habit was so bad that the staff sometimes put stiff plastic bibs on these children in order to preserve their clothing. The staff said that when Paul had been first admitted to the ward he did not chew his clothes, but started to do so about three months after his arrival. This suggests that, unoccupied and seated in a row with children who had long-established habits of chewing their clothes, Paul had copied the habit from them.

From observations of the children, it appeared that their odd habits might be strongly influenced by their environment. For example, 11-year-old Evelyn had two entirely different patterns of behaviour; one at her day school and the other in her ward. She was handicapped by the effects of rubella, and she had been in hospital for five years. She was deaf, had no speech and very little sight. She was ambulant, could feed herself, and sometimes was reliable about the toilet. Sometimes also she tried to help dress herself. There were 27 children in Evelyn's ward, all very disabled, and 21 were totally dependent on the nurses for all their care. Evelyn was the only child in her ward who was attending an outside special day-school (see p. 66): she went by taxi every day to a deaf/blind unit attached to a local deaf school about three miles from the hospital.

The following is a description of a typical day for Evelyn:

In the ward at 8.30am: Evelyn was ready to go to school. There were five nurses on duty, giving breakfast to the most disabled children and getting children ready for hospital school. Evelyn stood gyrating in a tiny circle on one spot in the middle of the ward. She held her head on one side, shook her head, and poked her right cheek and ear with her thumb. Once she stopped this gyrating and went into the bedroom where the spastic children were still being fed. She scraped her hands around the sticky, used bowls on the trolley, then sucked the cold porridge from her hands.

At 9.15: Evelyn's taxi came. On arrival at school, she had her coat taken off and was encouraged to feel the pegs where her coat was being hung. Then she stood by the teacher, feeling the teacher's skirt and knees. She bent down to pick up a small piece of cellophane paper; she held this and turned it over and over, perhaps attracted by its slight glitter. She did not move away from the teacher's knee.

The staff of Evelyn's unit were: two qualified teachers of the deaf, one classroom assistant, two classroom general helpers, and four houseparents. Nine children, aged between two and 11 years, attended the unit. Four were weekly boarders. All had visual, auditory and physical handicaps of varying degrees of severity. Two were non-ambulant, and two needed help with feeding. The nine children were given a great deal of personal attention because there were seven staff for the morning session of school and nine staff for the afternoon. Ever since Evelyn had started at the unit, 11 months earlier, she had been assigned one particular member of staff: a classroom helper named N.

104

From 9.45 until 11.45: N. worked continuously with Evelyn (with a break for the children's drinks half-way through the morning). Evelyn played with posting apparatus, matching shapes and crayoning. She was talked to, and encouraged to use her limited sight to sort out two colours. She did some speech-training work, although not yet showing any ability to produce meaningful sounds. She was also given a glockenspiel to play. Despite her hearing losses, she greatly enjoyed this musical instrument and it caused one of her rare smiles. The apparatus and toys that Evelyn was given were carefully interpreted for her by N., who held her hands and guided them over the objects and encouraged Evelyn to hold things up to her eyes. The pleasure she derived from the activities was obviously increased by the lively and kind way in which N. participated in all that Evelyn did with the apparatus.

At 11.45: Evelyn was encouraged to make an 'eat' sign, touching her mouth, then went to the table for lunch. After lunch she was shown how to take her empty plate to the kitchen and place it on the draining-board.

During the period immediately following lunch, and throughout the afternoon school session, Evelyn was constantly in close contact with the staff. She was encouraged to participate in play and paddling in the pool with the other children; she was taken for a short walk in the school grounds and given leaves to hold and feel, and practised going up and down the steps leading to the front door of the school. The staff were meticulous in interpreting her environment for her: for example, when she was taken into the lavatory she was encouraged to feel the lavatory seat, to pull up her own pants afterwards, wash her hands, feel the taps, notice the difference between hot and cold water, find the towel and smell the soap—and she was spoken to all the time. She showed trust in the staff, and obviously had an especially close and happy relationship with N. She showed no signs of peculiar behaviour patterns during her six hours in the school.

At 3.45pm: Evelyn arrived back in her ward. There were four staff on duty for the 27 children. Evelyn's coat was taken off as she walked into the ward, then she went to a chair and sat down. After a few minutes she got up and walked about the room. She found a chair with tubular steel legs and pushed it round and round in a small circle on one spot. The chair made a humming noise and Evelyn pressed her head on to the back of it to listen to this noise.

From 4 until 4.25: Evelyn alternately gyrated this chair or picked up small pieces of torn comic from the floor and flung them up in the air. Her feeding smock was put on her at 4.20, as she circled around the room.

From 4.25 until 4.55: She sat at the table and had her supper. Then she had her feeding smock taken off, and had a pair of pants put on her (her pants had previously dropped off soon after arriving back from school).

From 5 until 5.40: Evelyn again wandered about the room, mostly in circles; she picked up pieces of paper and threw them over her shoulder; pressed her thumb hard into her cheek, at the same time flapping her fingers and turning her head to one side. Sometimes she pushed a chair around to make the humming noise; sometimes she made a "dddd" noise as she pressed her thumb into her cheek.

At 5.40: She found a small cushion in a wheelchair. She walked about the room, repeatedly throwing this cushion over her shoulder and then turning around and picking it up again. She did this until 6.27, when she was taken to the lavatory by one of the nurses. She sat on the lavatory from 6.29 to 6.35.

From 6.35 until 6.55: Evelyn was being washed and put into her nightie.

Between 6.55 and 8.45: She was in the day-room, dressed in her nightie, and during this period she continuously circled around. Sometimes she threw the little cushion about, sometimes she made the humming noise with the spinning chair and pressed her ear to the back of it. Sometimes she flung little pieces of paper about. Sometimes she just stood circling in one spot in the middle of the room, digging her cheek with her thumb and saying "dddddd-dddddd".

At 8.41: She was taken to her bed.

At 8.45: She was in bed.

Evelyn received a total of 30 minutes human attention during five hours in the ward, and all that attention was concerned with her routine physical care. An analysis of the 30 minutes shows that she was touched seven times in the period from 3.45 to 8.45pm, for the following reasons:

(1) To have her coat taken off at 3.45 (half a minute).

(2) To have her feeding smock put on at 4.20 (one minute).

(3) To have a pair of pants put on, and her feeding smock taken off, at 5pm (two minutes).

(4) To be placed on the lavatory at 6.27 (two minutes).

(5) To be taken off the lavatory, washed, and changed into her nightie, from 6.35 to 6.55 (20 minutes).

(6) To be handed a drink by a nurse, at 7.45 (half a minute).

(7) To be put to bed, 8.41 until 8.45 (four minutes).

The remainder of her five hours was filled by: 3 hours 54 minutes tossing objects, humming the chair, gyrating in small circles and wandering about poking her cheek; 30 minutes sitting at the table, either eating or waiting to receive food; and six minutes sitting on the lavatory. The warmest moments of her five hours in the ward were when the night nurses put her to bed. This only took four minutes, but they did it with great kindliness, talking to her and holding her hand.

Repeated observations of Evelyn confirmed that she had a different pattern of behaviour for the two very different environments in which she was spending her life. In the ward, where her special needs as a child with sensory disabilities were not met and where the staff could not give her any attention except that needed to fulfil her basic physical needs, she had evolved a pattern of behaviour which provided some stimulation and structure for her existence. This perseverative, self-absorbing behaviour stopped when she was at school but was immediately resumed on her return to the ward. She made no effort to contact staff in the ward, and her expectations of receiving attention appeared to be very low. She showed no stress if visitors or staff made a fuss of other children.

106

When Evelyn was at school she received individual attention, play and affection. It appeared, too, that she had learnt to *expect* attention and affection, for she kept close to the staff and touched them, and she sometimes wept if N. gave attention to other children. Her hours in school were filled with activities which connected her to other people, and her surroundings were interpreted for her by staff who understood her sensory handicaps and were trying to develop her communication skills by using the correct aids (glasses, hearing-aids) and signs.

The nurses recognised that there were never enough staff in the ward to maintain the affectionate, individual attention that Evelyn received in school and which was necessary if she was to make progress. The Sister said: "We believe the school is helping her, but when she comes back to this environment she reverts to all her usual ways". Although her behaviour in the ward was strange, and completely different from how she behaved in school, it could not have been described as unhappy behaviour. She appeared to derive contentment from walking in circles, throwing cushions and paper, gyrating the chair and listening to its hum, and occasionally raking in soiled dishes for left-over food. However, lacking adult participation and guidance, her ward behaviour was solitary and perseverative, a mixture of stereotyped habits and tireless searches, concerned only with objects and devoid of any human involvement and communication. What she was doing in the ward might be described as a typical form of *institutional play*, derived by Evelyn herself from the meagre play-opportunities offered by her environment.

Many lonely institutional children play like Evelyn, and eventually their play becomes a series of apparently meaningless movements. It is difficult for the staff to sort out how much the queer patterns of behaviour are caused by mental handicap and how much by the hospital environment. As ward staff rarely have opportunities to observe the children away from the ward, many of them come to believe that peculiar behaviour patterns are entirely due to mental handicap.

Children's attempts to get attention and to form relationships with adults

Some of the children's habits were not only a source of self-occupation, but also a means of obtaining staff attention. 11-year-old Hugh, in hospital for 10 years, used to spend a lot of time lying on the floor in a small side-room, which usually had four or five children in it. Quite often there was no member of staff with these children. Hugh used to amuse himself by pulling small kitchen-type chairs onto his stomach and wriggling them up and down. He would also drag himself over to a cupboard and put his fingers under its door and open and shut it to make a loud bang. One of his commonest habits was to punch the wall with his clenched fist.

One day Hugh had been lying by the cupboard, opening and shutting its door, for some 10 minutes when one of the nurses came into the room and lifted another child, Eden, off the floor. The nurse sat on a sofa-swing and rocked back and forth with Eden on her lap. Hugh, seeing the happy time that the other child was having, swiftly dragged himself across the room, went behind the sofa and began to thump his clenched fist repeatedly on the glass of the french-doors. The nurse immediately went and picked up Hugh and laid him on the sofa with Eden, and then she rocked and cuddled them together. Observations over a number of weeks showed that Hugh often banged on the *wall* with his fist, but he only banged on *glass* when nurses were near him or when they were giving obvious attention to other children. He always got attention when he did this, either being picked up or grumbled at warningly about cutting himself. Another way in which Hugh got attention was to call "digger-digger-digger-bugger". This would usually make the staff laugh, and they would tickle him.

Some children failed miserably in their attempts to get attention. 13-year-old Kurt, in hospital for 11 years, used to crawl about his ward, going up to staff and holding out his hand to them and saying "'ere *yah*," but the only people who ever took any notice of him were new volunteers or visitors to the ward.

Children's relationships with staff were often made very insecure because of frequent changes of staff and the organisation of duty times. This insecurity was particularly noticeable in the case of 13-year-old Rachel, who had been in hospital since the age of seven. Because of hip deformities, Rachel had to spend her life lying on her back (see pp. 28-29). However, she had good hand ability and could feed herself with biscuits, chips, bananas and fish-fingers, and she could communicate by facial expression and with one or two single words; when asked if she wanted a banana, she would assent by smiling, nodding, holding out her hands and saying "mnn, yes".

The ward sister always made a special fuss of Rachel. One example of the sister's recognition of her individuality was to let her choose her own breakfast cereal; her latest favourite cereal would be put on the breakfast trolley and the sister would reassure her that she could have it. The pleasure Rachel obtained from choosing her own cereal was only one aspect of the positive relationship which had developed between her and the sister; it extended into other areas of care, such as bath-time and dressing, when Rachel chose her own talcum powder and her own dress to wear. However, the ward had constantly changing staff and there was often some confusion and unhappiness for Rachel when the sister was off duty. New and inexperienced staff did not always know about her choosing her own cereal, and they did not understand what Rachel was trying to signify by the unhappy looks she cast at the trolley if the favourite packet was not there. Then, when she cried at being given porridge, which she particularly hated, the inexperienced staff were inclined to grumble at her for making a noise and being fussy. This sort of unhappy situation might have been avoided if the organisation of the hospital had been oriented more towards encouraging the continuity of child/staff relationships, which is essential if speech-impaired and physically incapacitated children are to feel any security. One method of helping to encourage a more personal approach to the children would be to briefly list their individual preferences for food, clothes, method of bathing, position in the ward and so on, and make certain that all staff coming into the ward read the list and follow its advice.

The majority of the nurses were aware of the children's mothering and play needs and were worried at not being able to satisfy them, but there were a few who appeared to be insensitive to these needs. They not only failed to recognise the efforts that some of the children were making to play and to form relationships, but they also failed to recognise their own rôle in this sphere. The following record of five-year-old Peter's activities during one day indicates that his staff were missing many opportunities to mother him and to encourage his play development. Peter had been living for two years in Ash Hospital special-care ward, which accommodated 24 children aged from five to 21 years. He could move about by pushing with one hand on the floor, at the same time dragging himself along on his bottom.

8.40am: Breakfast had just finished. The six nurses on duty were wiping the children's faces. Peter was shuffling about the floor, picking up all the bits of dropped food he could find and eating them. He found a small piece of string, sat still and waved this about in front of him.

9am: Peter was trying to take off the shoes from children who were lying on the floor. He succeeded in removing a shoe from a big boy. He crouched by a chair and pushed the shoe round and round on the seat of it. One of the domestic staff began to wash the floor with a bucket of disinfectant water. Peter and some of the other children were soon lying in the dampness.

9.45: He was picked up by a nursing assistant, who said: "You're cheeky". She looked closely into his face for a minute and then turned to the other staff and said: "He'll be right ugly when he's older", then put him back on the floor.

10.05: Peter was shuffling around the room. He found a white comb, picked it up, sucked it, held it above his head, and then shuffled off again, holding it in one hand. He looked for other bits and pieces. He found a piece of squashed toast, which had been swirled around in the cleaner's mop, and ate it. He still kept hold of the white comb. As he explored, he managed to collect a red strap, a pink slipper and a toy rubber elephant. He tried to hold all these treasures, and the comb, in one hand against his chest, at the same time propelling himself along with the other hand. He had no special place in which to put these toys, and nobody noticed the difficulties that he was having in keeping his collection intact.

10.20: He had lost the pink slipper, the elephant and the white comb, having dropped them in his struggles to get along. But he still had the red strap, and he began to thread this through the foot-rest of a wheelchair.

10.55: A nurse gave Peter a drink, kneeling on the floor beside him where he was crouched by the wheelchair. The staff then stood by the day-room serving hatch, having their own mid-morning drinks.

11am: One of the other children slid open the door of the toy cupboard and started to throw out all the toys: a large, naked doll, plastic bricks, balls, a few soft toys and some screwed-up comics. A comic landed near Peter. He tore it up. Then he noticed a piece of string, picked it up and dragged it back and forth across the floor. 13-year-old Kurt crawled across to Peter and caught hold of the string. Peter tried to open Kurt's fingers and get the string back, but he was not strong enough. He looked towards the staff for help, cried, tried again to prise open Kurt's fingers, failed, and cried louder. The staff then got cross with Peter because he was making such a noise. Two nurses opened Kurt's fingers, rescued the string, flung it to Peter, and took Kurt across to the other side of the room and fastened him into a small chair against the wall. Peter shuffled rapidly off with his piece of string. The SEN said: "Somebody'll have to do something about that Peter, for his own good. He's getting really spoilt, he'll be a right pest on the wards if he's allowed to get away with it". The irritation of the staff appeared to be because Peter wanted to play and have attention and an adult to help him. He seemed to cause the staff far more worry than did those children who lay quietly sucking their clothes.

11.30: Peter was put into a cut-down high-chair to wait for his lunch. After he had been fastened into the chair he was given a squeaky toy to hold. He dropped it. He tried to get it, reaching his hand vainly towards where it lay on the floor, but could not reach it. He kicked angrily, reached his hand down again, grunted, then whimpered and looked around for help. Nobody responded. He kicked harder and whined loudly. A nurse said: "He's really getting spoilt, that child". Nobody picked up his toy or went to him. The nurses were preparing for lunch: some were putting children into chairs, others were laying the trolley, and some were chopping up food.

12.30pm: Lunch was finished. Peter was now sitting on the floor. Some of the children were having their faces wiped in the day-room, others were being taken to the bathroom. Peter was aimlessly flicking a piece of thin string about. He did not look happy. He shuffled up to where I was sitting and looked up at me. He held up the string. I found a paper towel in my pocket, rolled this into a ball, tied in onto the string and dragged it along for him. He stretched out his hands for it. He crawled away with it and found a chair with a foot-rest and threaded the ball and string through the foot-rest; then he lay on the floor, holding the end of the string and watching the paper ball bob up and down and swing from side to side as he moved the string. After about six minutes the paper ball fell off the string. Peter immediately shuffled back to me and held up the ball and string for me to put them together again. Then he went away and continued playing with it once more under the chair. After a while he tangled the string around the foot-rest, and just as he was successfully managing to disentangle it the chair was suddenly pushed to one side by one of the passing nurses. He cried bitterly at the disappearance of his plaything. A student nurse, who had just come on duty, returned the chair to him and helped him to untangle his string. She was making a special study of Peter as part of her training, and she took a particular interest in him.

12.45: The student nurse played with Peter and his string for a few minutes.

1pm: One of the nurses went off duty, leaving five nurses on the ward for the rest of the day.

2.30: Peter was hanging his ball and string over the seats of chairs.

3pm: Peter was upset and crying loudly because his paper ball had again come off the string. The staff once more referred to him as 'spoilt'. They appeared unable to appreciate how important his plaything was to him.

3.15: Having cried for a while, Peter was picked up by his student. She sat cuddling him. The older nurses told the student that she would 'ruin' Peter, and said "he's naughty today because you took him home with you yesterday". They talked for a while about how necessary it was to "make the children behave, as it saves trouble later on when they've grown up and are on the adult wards". The general feeling among the older nurses in Peter's ward was that giving attention to the children was: "making a rod for your own back"; "not fair to other staff, as the children get difficult when you're not there"; "all the children have to be treated alike"; and "it is bad to get emotionally involved with the children". Nurses who were interested in mothering the children, especially student nurses, found these attitudes difficult to combat.

3.45: One of the nurses walked around the room with a plate of banana sandwiches, feeding some of the children who were on the floor. Peter called out and stretched up his hands and tried to take a sandwich from the plate. The nurse said: "He only has to see me with a plate and he makes noises and tries to grab the sandwiches, he is very greedy". She seemed unable to accept that his calls were not just greediness but perhaps a stage in his attempts to communicate, and that his wish to take a sandwich from the plate himself might be regarded as a positive sign of progress. The student nurse took a sandwich for him, sat him on her lap and fed him.

6.05: Supper time. The student tried to teach Peter to hold his spoon and feed himself. Then she was told to leave him and take one of the older boys into the bedroom and get him ready for bed. The SEN then fed Peter, holding the dish and spoon above his head, and rapidly spooning his pudding into his mouth. She went into the bedroom and told the student how quickly Peter had eaten his supper.

6.45: The only children still in the day-room were Peter and five-year-old Anne. Peter was sitting on the floor, crying.

All the observations undertaken in Peter's ward appeared to indicate a considerable lack of understanding about the children's mothering and play needs. This was especially obvious in the constant references the staff made to children being 'spoilt' if they wanted attention.

Peter, being mobile, could shuffle about and make his presence felt, albeit it made him rather unpopular. It was difficult for the less mobile children to assert themselves, but some were acute observers of staff moving about and were unhappy if placed in positions where they could not watch this activity. In Larch Hospital special-care ward 11-year-old Florence (see p. 101) liked to watch the nurses going in and out of the bathroom, and the domestic staff as they washed the windows or floor, and she would try to catch the glances of staff and smile at them. One afternoon she was put in her wheelchair at 1.30,

111

in a quiet part of the ward where there was no adult for her to watch. She occupied herself by twiddling the screws of her wheelchair and sucking her fingers. At 3.40 a domestic worker came into that section of the ward, picked up one of the younger children and sat cuddling her near Florence's chair. Florence immediately stretched out her hands towards the domestic worker's back and pulled at the apron belt until she managed to untie it. The domestic worker said "Look at naughty old Florence" and turned around and smiled at her. Florence smiled back, said "oh, oh, oh" in an excited manner and tried to hold the domestic worker's hands. Her outgoing liveliness at this opportunity to involve herself with an adult was in stark contrast to the inward-looking and limited behaviour she had been exhibiting during the previous two hours, when no adult had been near.

Sometimes the most severely disabled children, whose movements and hand abilities were extremely limited and who had no speech, made attempts to obtain attention and to join in some adult activity, but their meagre movements were simply not noticed. The following observations of 10-year-old Emma are an example of this. Emma had very severe physical disabilities which prevented her from moving easily, and she had been living for seven years in Larch Hospital special-care ward (which accommodated 27 children). The children had been divided into two groups, one consisting of children who had some abilities such as crawling or manoeuvring their wheelchairs, the other of children who were almost totally incapacitated. Emma and 14 other children were in the latter group. They spent their time in a small partitioned-off section of the main ward, where they were safe from the 12 more mobile children who might have run their wheelchairs over their faces or hands. The nurses of this ward were exceptionally gentle and kind to all the children, but because of pressure of work, these 15 most disabled children were often left alone for very long periods in their quiet section of the ward.

1.30pm: Emma was lying quietly on a mattress, watching the end of the room where she occasionally saw a nurse walk past, or a volunteer pushing one of the more able children up and down in a wheelchair.

2pm: Two visitors arrived to see Lane, another of the children in Emma's section. Emma looked up at the visitors as they passed her mat and said "ah-ah-ah-ah", but they did not notice her. They sat down on two kitchen-type chairs by the french-windows, cuddled Lane and opened parcels. Emma's face brightened as she heard the crackling paper. Interested in what the visitors were doing she began to kick her way towards them. By making great efforts, kicking with one foot and then sliding slowly along on her side, she managed to manoeuvre herself off the mattress and along the floor.

3pm: Emma managed to reach Lane's visitors. It had taken her 30 minutes of determined kicking to drag herself approximately 10 feet. She stopped by Lane's visitors and watched them. They continued to rustle their parcels. They did not take any notice of Emma, although by now she was almost under their chairs. They were a sad couple, and generally tried to avoid seeing the other

112

children when they visited their own child. They came twice a week, usually bringing parcels of clothes or food, and Emma always enjoyed watching them.
3.10: Emma managed to get herself behind one of the visitor's chairs. She raised herself on her elbows to look out of the french-windows into the courtyard, where leaves were blowing about noisily. The sound of rustling leaves, like paper, always interested her.
3.15: A nurse came into this section of the ward and saw Emma lying by the window. She caught hold of her by one foot and pulled her back onto the mattress where she had previously been lying before Lane's visitors had come. The nurse had not been deliberately unkind, she was simply unaware that Emma had taken 30 minutes to travel the short distance to watch the visitors. Emma lay face-down on the mattress. Suddenly, a stronger wind whipped up the leaves in the courtyard, and she raised herself on her elbow and tried to lift her head to see what was going on.
3.25: Lane's visitors took him out for a walk. Justin's mother arrived in the ward. She sat at the far end of Emma's section and took Justin onto her lap. Emma, having now lost Lane's visitors and hearing Justin's mother, but not being in a position to see her, began to get agitated. She made protest noises and tried to turn herself around to see Justin's mother. She did not succeed. She subsided into a face-down position, and began her comfort habit of sucking the two middle fingers of her right hand.
3.40: Lane's visitor's came back, and sat down by the window again. Emma lifted her head and brightened up. She took her fingers from her mouth, and watched the visitors.

This record of Emma's behaviour shows how the efforts she had made to be part of the adult scene failed to attract the attention of either the staff or the visitors. Her failure was understandable, because it is sometimes difficult to see any purpose in the meagre movements of multiply handicapped children. However, a great deal of their behaviour does make sense: for example Emma's apparently meaningless babblings and threshings about ceased to be meaningless when there was time to notice her vocalisations and movements in the context of what was taking place in the immediate environment. She made the "ah-ah" noise when the visitors arrived and straightaway began her slow kicking movements towards them. Her behaviour may be likened to that of any young child who is pleased to see visitors and wants to see what they have brought. A non-handicapped child in that situation may have said a clear "hello" and run up to visitors in less than a minute, but because Emma could neither speak nor walk she merely appeared to be making unintelligible noises and meaningless movements for 30 minutes.

Variations in amount of mothering attention given to individual children
Observations of the 223 children indicated that all could be described as underprivileged in the amounts of mothering and play they received. The amount of mothering attention being given to the children averaged only five

minutes each in 10 hours (see p. 100). However, it was noticed that 28 of the 223 children consistently received *more* than this, perhaps between 20 and 60 minutes of mothering attention in 10 hours. This extra attention seemed to be influenced by the following 11 identifiable characteristics and abilities, of which each of the 28 more 'privileged' children had at least five:

(1) Attractive features: no outstandingly obvious facial scars, deformities or skin disease (26 children).

(2) Good family contact (25 children).

(3) Ability to grasp with hands (24 children).

(4) Ability to make eye-contact (24 children).

(5) Aged under 13 years (23 children).

(6) Small size (16 children).

(7) Mobility: ability to bottom-shuffle, crawl, walk or manoeuvre a wheelchair (16 children).

(8) Had lived at home for the first five years of life (15 children).

(9) Ability to feed themselves (12 children).

(10) Some language ability: repeat a phrase, say "hello" (nine children).

(11) Less than five years in hospital (15 children).

This observation suggests that a child's chances of receiving extra attention were influenced by how much feed-back he was able to give his staff. Factors which appeared to be most important to feed-back were the child having an attractive face, being able to make eye-contact, and being able to grasp (*i.e.* perhaps being able to take an offered toy, hold hands, or help with dressing oneself).

However, a study of the patterns of attention-giving in long-stay wards indicate more than the obvious fact that a pretty child who gives the staff some satisfactory feed-back is likely to get attention. Another significant factor was that regular family visiting influenced the amount of attention the children received: *i.e.* 25 of the 28 children who got extra attention from the staff had good family contact and were regularly visited. It might be that families continued to keep in good contact with these particular children because they, like the staff, appreciated the feed-back that a child with attractive features, good eye-contact and the ability to use his hands was able to give. However, it is also possible that regular family contact was a positive influence on the child's *ability to maintain the means of attracting attention, i.e.* family contact nurtured his social development.

The facts of having been at home for at least the first five years of life and in hospital for less than five years also seemed to influence the children's receipt of attention. This suggests that early admission to and long periods in an institution are factors which are likely to reduce the child's ability to obtain attention from his staff. It was particularly noticeable that children who had had the benefit of family life for at least their first five years appeared to be more socially competent (*i.e.* were able to attract attention and give satisfaction) than those who had been admitted to the institution in early childhood. The circumstances of Arthur and Vince, both of whom received more than average attention from their staff, support this theory. The family life-styles of both these boys had been very similar: although they were non-ambulant and speechless, they had both been at the centre of affectionate family life, had been included in all outings and were accustomed to neighbours and relatives visiting their homes.

Fourteen-year-old Arthur had been admitted to Elm Hospital when he was 11 years old. He was very competent at making eye-contact and had a quick sense of humour; he laughed at appropriate times and his smiles were appreciated by the ward staff. He vocalised in a meaningful way, and the staff described him as "knowing what was what". He was usually placed in a central position in the ward, where he could see everything going on and receive attention from passing staff and visitors. 14-year-old Vince had been admitted to Birch Hospital at the age of 10 years, and he also had positive relationships with the staff. He was particularly vocal, and this was said to be because when he was at home his mother used to put him in the hall when she was doing her housework upstairs; she kept up a shouting conversation with him as she worked, and encouraged him to shout up the stairs to her. Vince was adept at shouting to the staff when they were working in other parts of the ward, and he could make sounds which resembled "hello" and "bye-bye".

An example of how variations in the children's receipt of attention might be related to the length of time they had been in hospital was seen in Ward 11 of Pine Hospital. Nine of the 17 children in Ward 11 were receiving minimal attention, and although four of these nine had not been admitted to hospital until the age of five or over, all four had subsequently spent between nine and 15 years in hospital (Table VI). One might speculate whether these four children had, on admission, possessed the ability to attract attention but had lost it during their subsequent years in hospital, or whether all multiply handicapped children, regardless of their age at admission, have particular problems in obtaining attention as they reach late adolescence.

Another interesting point in Table VI is that while Clive and Irene had both been admitted at seven years of age and had both spent five years in the hospital, Clive received extra attention, while Irene received minimal attention. The difference in the backgrounds of these two children was that Clive had lived with foster-parents until the age of seven, while Irene had lived in a residential nursery for retarded children since babyhood.

Giving attention to blind children

Special concern should be felt for the situation of blind or partially sighted children, for they appeared to be particularly at risk of lack of attention, especially as they reached adolescence. In addition to lacking attention in their wards, they were also liable to be excluded from full-time education, and they attracted no attention from volunteers. Throughout the ward observations, it was noticed that the blind or partially sighted adolescents who were non-ambulant, unvisited, and had been in the institution for many years, lay very still and quiet. They vocalised scarcely at all, they did not stretch out their hands, and barely even moved their fingers. Their hands were often curled into useless shapes and their heads were in fixed positions. They were too heavy to lift up and cuddle, and appeared to be at special risk of social isolation. Unable to make eye-contact, they had nothing to compensate them socially for their increasing loss of physical movement and lack of personal appeal.

In all the hospitals visited there seemed to be a need for staff to be given special guidelines on the care of blind, non-ambulant children in institutions, which would carefully spell out that these children need to receive very frequent opportunities for sustained human contact at all ages. Such guidelines would stress the blind children's need to be touched, moved, cuddled, spoken to, and to have objects put into their hands and to have their hands held by the staff. Particular attention needs to be given to their hands, because these are the only means of social contact for children who are blind, speechless and non-ambulant, and if their hands are allowed to atrophy then their social isolation is increased. Care should also be taken not to leave blind, non-ambulant children in their wheelchairs in corners of the room, but to place them always within touching and hearing distance of other children and adults, and within sound of whatever activities are going on. Even if a ward is very under-staffed and the only activities are domestic ones, the blind, non-ambulant child might still profitably be placed in a position where passing staff can touch him, feel his hands and encourage him to make sounds and to stretch out his hands.

TABLE VI

Pattern of attention-giving in a long-stay ward

Child	Age (yrs)	Age when admitted to hospital (yrs)	No. of years in hospital	Mothering and play attention given by ward staff
Barbara	8	5	5	More than average*
Kenneth	9	7	2	More than average
Rose	10	7	3	More than average
Nora	10	8	2	More than average
Enoch	11	< 1	11	Less than average
Joseph	11	5	6	More than average
Clive †	12	7	5	More than average
Emily	12	< 1	12	Less than average
Irene ‡	12	7	5	Less than average
Betty	15	10	5	More than average
Phyllis	15	9	6	More than average
Nancy	18	3	15	Less than average
David	18	5	13	Less than average
Nita	18	8	10	Less than average
Olwen	19	7	12	Less than average
Keith	19	10	9	Less than average
Richard	20	1	19	Less than average

*Average is taken as five minutes mothering attention in 10-hour period.
† Admitted from a foster-home.
‡ Admitted from a residential nursery.

116

Children as 'entertainers'

Some of the attention given to the children took a form which appeared to be of doubtful value to the children. For instance those children who were getting extra attention were frequently looked upon as 'entertainers'. Eight-year-old Simon, in hospital since the age of four, with some speech and the ability to manoeuvre his wheelchair, was an 'entertainer'. He had been taught to say 'quaint' things, such as "does your hubby get drunk?", "how many pints did you have?" and "were you drunk last night?". Simon was sometimes kept up late because the night staff found his sayings amusing. Eight-year-old Joan was another typical 'entertainer'. She had been in hospital since babyhood and was often described by the nurses as being "a staff child, she wouldn't fit in anywhere except this hospital, she belongs to the staff". She was ambulant and had some speech, mostly catch-phrases such as "steak-and-beans". She would stand at the serving hatch with the staff as they had their coffee-breaks, and they would give her spoonfuls of coffee and pieces of sandwich. This homely scene was often spoiled because Joan was encouraged to take part in adult conversations and repeat phrases such as "did her husband beat her then?" in order to make the staff laugh. This type of attention-giving appeared to be encouraging the more able children to grow up with a smattering of meaningless joke phrases, which they did not understand but continuously repeated as a means of earning a cuddle, tickle or smile from staff and visitors.

It could be said that this attention was innocent and positive, and similar to the adult/child interaction that takes place in families when a toddler is taught to say something funny to amuse the adults. However, such relationships between the staff and long-stay hospital children is generally non-productive because the ward children, unlike normal toddlers in a family setting, are less likely to grow out of their funny catch-phrase stage and are at risk of regressing into mere clowns or parrots because their small abilities are not being developed for any purpose other than to entertain the constantly changing staff. This type of attention might have had some value in that it did at least encourage some form of human interaction for a few of the children, which was infinitely more positive than the social isolation suffered by the majority. Children who were entertainers often enjoyed a certain status in their wards: for example they sometimes helped to carry on their wheelchairs a bundle of pillow-cases from the linen cupboard to the bedroom, or they were taken to the shoe-repair shop to fetch shoes, or on similar trips to some other department in the hospital. They were usually the only children to be introduced to official visitors to the ward, and their names were the first that new staff learnt.

This tendency for staff to treat two or three children as entertainers was typical of all the special-care wards: for instance there was always a small group of 'star' children near the source of staff activities — by the door of sister's office, or by the serving hatch between the day-room and kitchen, where the staff would stand having coffee and looking at the newspaper. These star children would have manoeuvred their wheelchairs or crawled to these key places. Further down the room, furthest away from adult activities, there would be a large group of ignored, speechless, immobile children lying on mats or mattresses, or in bean-bags, or sitting in wheelchairs or small armchairs (see diagram on facing page).

It is important that staff be aware of the phenomenon of using some children as entertainers, and try to prevent the formation of these elitist groups, who not only deplete the amount of attention available to less able children, but also receive a doubtful quality of attention themselves. What was happening in the wards was not caused by unkindness on the part of the staff, but by a lack of guidelines which might have helped them to develop insight into the children's and their own behaviour.

The development of a specially favoured group might be prevented by:
(1) Staff understanding the importance of giving attention to *all* the children.
(2) Staff realising that if children are left in corners they are likely to withdraw and develop self-absorbing habits.
(3) Staff listing and discussing the special needs of children who might be particularly vulnerable to lack of attention, *i.e.* the blind adolescents.
(4) Staff making definite attempts to introduce *all* the children to new members of staff, so that new staff do not immediately fall into the habit of only giving attention to the more outstanding children.
(5) Staff appraising the usefulness to a child of being treated as an entertainer, *i.e.* how far is he being helped to develop reliable, lasting relationships with adults, or how far being exploited and encouraged to behave in a shallow, meaningless manner which will only emphasize his mental handicap and social incompetence.

The children's interaction with each other

Because of their severe physical, sensory and mental handicaps these were all essentially solitary children, but their solitariness was perhaps exacerbated by the ward organisation. For example many children were frequently anchored all day in wheelchairs, bean-bags or small armchairs, and so had no opportunities for social interaction. The staff did not always seem aware that the ward environment might cause isolation: they did not try to encourage social interaction by different methods of grouping the children, and they did not organise any group-play or have any policy of encouraging the children to interact with each other. It was noticeable that the staff were rarely involved in any social interaction that did take place between the children.

As mentioned earlier, the typical ward scene was that the star children were near the centre of adult activities, at the serving hatch or at the door of the sister's office, while the more disabled and ignored children would be further down the ward. The children in the armchairs, bean-bags and wheelchairs at the end of the room were not only isolated from staff activities, they were also unable to reach out and touch other children or see each other's faces very easily. It was not surprising that these children eventually reverted to self-absorbing habits such as playing with their hands and chewing their

118

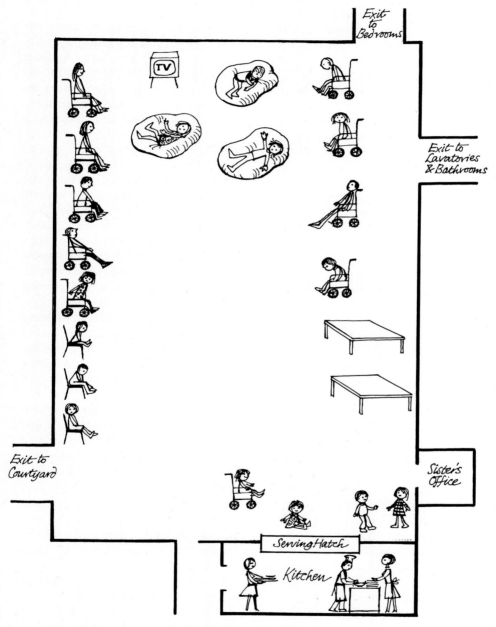

Exit to
Bedrooms

Exit to
Lavatories
& Bathrooms

TV

Exit to
Courtyard

Sister's
Office

Sewing Hatch

Kitchen

A typical ward scene.

119

jumpers. However, they were evidently aware of each other, for when a new child joined the group he was likely to learn the habits of other children in his row (*e.g.* Paul, see pp. 103-104).

It would seem that to get multiply handicapped children up from the floor and into small armchairs, which has been part of the 'up-grading' policy in mental handicap hospitals in recent years, may actually be restricting their social development in a way which was not envisaged by planners of the hospitals' environment. There has been tremendous financial expenditure on large bean-bags and small armchairs, but these have not really helped the children socially, although such items of furniture may appear to provide a pleasant 'home-like' environment.

In the wards where the children *were* able to touch each other, it was possible to observe what might be described broadly as infantile social interaction. This was particularly noticeable in Larch Hospital, where the most severely disabled children sometimes spent time lying all together on two mattresses on the floor. These children were able to wriggle and kick and stretch out their hands, and they pulled at each other's clothes, hair, hands and feet. They vocalised as they did so, and some made protest noises as they were touched, while others laughed as they caught hold of each other's hands.

The following two extracts from Larch Hospital observations are examples of the social interaction between some children who were free to touch each other.

1.15pm: Lunch was finished. There were six children on the mat, aged from four to 10. All were speechless, non-ambulant and severely handicapped. No staff were with them. Emma had her arm around Florence's legs. Florence lay on her side near Caroline's legs. All the children wore brightly-coloured tights, but no shoes. Florence played with Caroline's tights, pulling at their heels, and smiling.

1.30pm: A nurse picked up Caroline and took her to be changed. Florence still clutched Carolines' tights in her right hand, and as Caroline was picked up, Florence kept hold of the heel of the tights and they were stretched to about 18 inches before she let go. Florence smiled. After Caroline had been changed she was brought back and put beside Florence on the mat again, and Florence smiled at her. The nurse then picked up Florence and took her across to another mat and laid her over a foam rubber wedge. Florence whimpered and looked across to Caroline, but the nurse did not notice Florence's sad reaction to her removal from Caroline's mat. The staff had very little time to notice the possible development of friendships between the children, so they were likely accidently to separate children who were relating to each other.

The following interaction took place between two blind boys, aged seven and 10, both of whom had been in Larch hospital for three years. They were lying together on a mat.

Justin put his legs right across Stuart's face and chest and lay there for five minutes, quite still, then he rolled off. Stuart, stretching out his hand, found Justin's hand and held it, but Justin wriggled out of Stuart's way. Stuart groped and found Justin's hand again, then as Justin slipped once more out of his reach, Stuart caught hold of the cuff of Justin's jumper. There was a lot more wriggling between the two of them, some laughter, kicking of each other's faces, more laughter. Then for three minutes they lay still. Olive, a sighted child, aged four, disturbed by all this romping on her mat, dragged herself slowly off and sat on the lino. Emma, also on the mat, began to kick herself around in a circle. Justin said "oh - m m m m" and Stuart said "oh - d d d". Justin rolled over and came face to face with Queenie, aged eight. Their faces were almost touching. Queenie, attracted by the nearness of Justin's face, smiled directly at him. Blind, he did not respond to her smile. She smiled again. About ten minutes later, after a period of quiet, Stuart and Justin again began to enjoy some movement together. They were lying fairly close together, and Stuart was sucking his thumb, but with his left hand he felt about and, finding Justin's foot, he began to pull off Justin's sock. This action sparked off a lot of reaction from Justin: he laughed, shouted "hey-hey, hey-hey", and wriggled out of Stuart's reach altogether.

This very simple interaction between the children, little more than ticklings, wrigglings and touchings, might be described as so socially unsophisticated that it would lead nowhere developmentally. However, it is important to note that the children who were free on these mats did not have the solitary habits of the children who were always confined to bean-bags, wheelchairs and armchairs, e.g. continuously sucking hands and chewing clothes.

There were other advantages in the children being within reach of each other. They could at least have some chance of human contact with each other if the staff were unable to give them attention, and their freedom also encouraged them to be physically active and to vocalise. Several expressive sounds could be distinguished during their wrigglings, such as contentment when lying close beside another child, or protest noises when roughly rolled across or when trapped by another child's legs.

It was interesting to note that although Stuart and Justin were both blind and non-ambulant, they were physically very lively when they were free on the mat and within touching distance of other children. They enjoyed using their hands to seek out other children, and their lively behaviour was in marked contrast to the passive behaviour of older blind children who had been in hospital for many years, who were always confined to chairs and who seemed to have long lost all ability to stretch out their hands or to vocalise (see pp. 115-116). However, although the children were so active when they were on the mats together, they also became quiet and still and were inclined to perseverative habits whenever they were confined to chairs. For example it was not uncommon for Florence, who so much appreciated contact with adults and other children, to spend many hours in her wheelchair in a quiet part of the ward, and at these times she would just sit and twiddle the screws on the chair (see pp. 101, 111-112).

It was noticed in Bay Hospital that when 14-year-old Sally was confined to

121

her wheelchair she would sit sucking and chewing the straps of the chair for many hours (see p. 103), but when she was free to move about on the floor she would sometimes approach other children and seemed to be making attempts to play with them. Following is a description of Sally's behaviour one day when she was on the floor.

It was 1pm: Sally, in her wheelchair, was put into a small room adjoining the day-room, with six other children. No member of staff was with the children. A mentally handicapped woman from another ward, who used to help on the children's wards, was assigned to look after the group of children in this small room. Sally restlessly chewed the straps of her chair, and her dress, and fidgeted about in the chair as if trying to get out. The mentally handicapped woman took no notice of any of the children; she sat dozing on a mat.

At 1.30pm, Sally managed to free herself from her wheelchair; she slowly got down onto the floor and then rolled across the room. She found a sock, then lay on the floor and held the sock above her face, tickled her face with it and laughed. Then she twice banged her head on the floor. 10-year-old Hugh lay in the middle of the floor. He had no socks on, his trousers and nappy had slipped down. He held up one hand above his head, almost motionless. Sally rolled over and over across the room, and cuddled Hugh for three minutes. He laughed, and put his hand down onto his chest. He looked around for her when she rolled away again.

Sally then rolled across to a plastic settee. She rubbed her hands backwards and forwards on it, making a squeaky noise on the plastic seat. She did this for one minute. Then she rolled across to a large ball which was standing in the corner of the room: she pulled this on top of her body and bounced it on her chest for a moment. Then again she went to Hugh. She pulled him by his jumper and poked her fingers inquisitively at his eyes. Hugh was now very soiled, and with his trousers and nappy around his knees, his very dirty bottom and back were exposed to view. Sally rolled up to the mentally handicapped woman who was dozing on the mat. Sally held her hand for a moment, but received no response from her. Hugh tried to pull up his trousers and nappy with one hand. He could not manage this difficult task, and his efforts caused his nappy to come completely out of his plastic pants. He bit the back of his hand angrily. (Hugh's hand was bruised and scarred by the constant frustrated bitings it received when he failed to achieve the things that he wanted to do.) As Hugh bit his hand, Sally went to him and she cuddled him and stroked his face. She behaved as if wanting to comfort him. He stroked her face also, and looked up at her and said "gedder-gedder-gedder" in a high voice. She saw a small piece of blanket lying on the floor, and she tried to cover his face with this. He laughed.

Sally then went to the wall mirror. She looked at herself in the mirror and tapped her reflection with her fingers. Soon afterwards the nurses came into the room and Sally was returned to her wheelchair.

The children from Larch Hospital and Bay Hospital who have been described in the last few pages were all very severely handicapped, but it would seem that they *were* capable of making attempts to interact socially if they were free to do so, although their attempts were very infantile and perhaps not very noticeable. Even if the children were not free on mats but merely had their chairs in a circle instead of in a straight row, so that they could touch each other, then they sometimes reached out and held each other's hands or head or hair, or put their hands on each other's knees. This need to have human contact appeared to be very important to them.

One Sunday afternoon in Birch Hospital, 26-year-old Des, 19-year-old Laura and 11-year-old Alice were able to play together because their wheelchairs were place at angles to one another. Laura held a pink plastic toy on her lap. She held it very tightly. Des leaned from his chair and gently tried to take it from her but she would not let it go. He held the toy and her hand together, and shook her hand slowly up and down. Laura smiled and gave a slight shriek, but still did not let go of the toy. Then Alice leaned from her wheelchair and also tried to get hold of the toy, at the same time patting her hand up and down on Laura's lap. None of this behaviour was aggressive. This game between the three young people lasted for 16 minutes, and only stopped when the nurses had to move their chairs for tea-time.

It is desirable that staff encourage more of the infantile social interaction described in the previous pages by grouping the children more thoughtfully and by avoiding isolating the children in bean-bags and in rows of wheelchairs and armchairs. If chairs and wheelchairs were arranged in clusters of three or four so that the children were able to reach each other, and if the children had periods on the floor together and were encouraged to romp, then perhaps some of the withdrawal and self-absorbing habits might be prevented. Such an approach, aiming at developing social interaction between the children, might also be more rewarding for the staff than seeing the children merely sitting in rows and chewing their clothes.

While the most severely handicapped children's attempts to interact socially were so meagre as to be hardly noticeable, the less handicapped children made more obvious contact with other children. For example some of the more able, older children showed affection for the youngest of the most handicapped children, and would kiss and cuddle them and stroke their faces. A few of the more able children were inclined to behave in a chastising manner towards the less able; for example, in Birch Hospital, 16-year-old Donald would manoeuvre his wheelchair about the room and grumble at the less able children who were chewing their clothes. One day Donald went into the day-room and found Laura waving a book about, which her family had just given her when they had visited. She had been sitting in her chair for eight minutes waving this book about in one hand and occasionally chewing the corners of it. When Donald saw the book he made a dash towards Laura and snatched it from her. She made no protest, but just looked vaguely sad and continued to wave her now empty hand. Donald looked closely at the chewed corners of the book, frowned, then tucked it away down the side of his wheelchair and moved away. In Donald's ward there was one girl who was a particularly chronic clothes-chewer, and she was frequently grumbled at by the staff for chewing holes in the front of her jumper. Donald would often go up to her, poke her in the chest and say "Don't like her, don't like her". She never took any notice of him or his poking.

Social interaction among the most mobile children, especially those who were 'stars', was often aggressive. They would snatch each other's belongings and rattle each other's wheelchairs very roughly. These children would often ignore each other for long periods, then suddenly come together, engage in some poking, pushing and snatching pattern of behaviour, momentarily annoy and upset each other, and then abruptly move away again. This momentary play usually lasted little more than five or six minutes. The following extract from ward observations illustrates the typical behaviour of a group of star children in Pine Hospital:

It was 6pm. Six children were in the day-room, two of whom were quiet, withdrawn, ignored children. The other four were ward 'stars'. The staff and the rest of the children were in the bathroom. The star children were: 15-year-old Phyllis, six years in hospital, ambulant; 11-year-old Joseph, six years in hospital, able to manoeuvre his wheelchair; 10-year-old Nora, two years in hospital, ambulant; and nine-year-old Kenneth, two years in hospital, ambulant.

I was sitting on a chair by the window. Phyllis and Nora came and sat down on either side of me, and Joseph manoeuvred his wheelchair so that he was by my knee. Although the star children never received much response from me, they usually congregated around me when the staff were in the bathroom. They had established a habit of keeping near any adult in the room. Phyllis suddenly screwed up my notebook, then stood up and slapped Joseph in the face, took hold of his wheelchair and rattled and shook it back and forth very violently. Nora giggled hysterically at the noise of Joseph's chair being rattled so hard by Phyllis.

Kenneth came over and stood near Nora. He was holding a small rubber table-mat. He liked these mats and would often take one off the table after supper and walk about the day-room rolling it backwards and forwards under his chin and pressing it against his face. Phyllis stopped shaking Joseph's chair and sat down beside me again. Kenneth stood staring at Nora. Suddenly Joseph stretched out his hand and snatched Kenneth's table-mat. Kenneth cried. Phyllis jumped up, swung Joseph's wheelchair swiftly around and shoved it into the middle of the room. Joseph showed no fear. Kenneth crossed the room and made a grab for his mat, but Joseph hung on to it very tightly. Nora jumped up and joined in grabbing for the mat, and Phyllis ran across and rattled Joseph's chair. It was now a tug-of-war between Nora, Joseph and Kenneth, with all three clinging on to the mat, and Phyllis continuing to shove Joseph's wheelchair backwards and forwards very hard.

After a few moments Kenneth moved away, Nora and Phyllis came and sat down by me again, and Joseph remained in the middle of the room. The mat remained on Joseph's lap.

Although there were these occasional incidents of sudden fighting amongst the more able children, most of their play was solitary and usually consisted of carrying a shoe or an empty carrier-bag or 'Kleenex' box about the room; or they merely stood about the door of the sister's office, or the serving hatch, waiting for some attention from the staff.

Toys

In several of the wards the toys consisted only of a few naked, limbless dolls, torn comics, pieces of broken plastic toys, plastic hammers, toy shopping-baskets and 'Maxi-bricks'. But in other hospitals a lot of money seemed to have been spent on expensive toys and play equipment: for example in one hospital, accommodating more than 1000 patients, it was said that £1000 a year for the last four years had been allocated to buying toys. In the special-care ward of that hospital there was a barrel full of plastic toys and some musical instruments, and two life-size, furry lion cubs. These two lions, sitting just inside the day-room door, appeared to serve little purpose except as grotesque ornaments in the very deprived environment of that particular ward.

The special-care ward in another hospital had recently had a playroom built onto it, costing £10,000. Of this sum, £200 had gone towards equipping the room with toys. There was a little slide, a small wooden pram, one or two 'sense-training' toys, and a sand-tray. But these toys were kept in an inner cupboard in the new playroom, and the room itself was being used merely as an extension of the rather bare day-room. The more mobile children would roam about it during the evenings, sometimes pushing empty wheelchairs up and down.

In another special-care ward, a side room had been made into a small playroom and had been equipped with beautifully made wooden trains, cars, lorries, and a sand-tray and water-tray. However, the room was not used because there were not enough staff to spare two nurses to take a group of children into the room and help them to play.

Some of the ward sisters kept a small store of 'sense-training' toys in their offices, and occasionally these would be brought out and given to one of the more able children, who would be sat at a table to play with them for a while. These formal toys were usually very boring for the child and he would be apathetic in his response to them.

Most of the wards had mobiles, plastic toys and soft toys hanging on strings from the ceiling. These often made a very colourful display and some of the children would watch them as they slowly gyrated in the heat which rose from the room. But hanging toys, no matter how attractive, do not help children to build up relationships with other human beings.

Although there was a variety of toys in the special-care wards, varying from expensive, outsize cuddly toys to formal 'sense-training' apparatus and toys spinning on strings from the ceiling, there was really very little under-standing about the meaning of play and the use of toys for multiply handicapped children. It seemed to be thought that it was enough to surround the children with bright objects, but a child could be surrounded by many colourful toys and remain impassive, with blank expression and still hands, until a member of staff came and sat with him and touched him; only then would he smile, move his hands and vocalise.

It is possible that money is being wasted on purchasing toys which pay lip-service to the idea of play in hospital, but do nothing to help the staff and the children develop a warm relationship. There seems to be little point in buying toys for multiply handicapped children unless the toys are going to actively encourage some close personal interaction between the staff and children, or between the children themselves.

Many of the children who made no response to soft or plastic toys did seem to enjoy listening to small musical boxes tied to their cots or wheelchairs, which could be played to them by passing staff. For example Emma had a small television toy tied to one side of her cot, which livened up her evenings after she had been put to bed. When it was wound up it played a tune and a moving picture passed along its screen. However, it seemed that much of Emma's pleasure in this toy lay in the attention from staff it brought her. The staff would run laughing across the bedroom to turn it on again for her when it had finished running, and she would smile and wave her hands as she watched them.

The mobile children usually appeared to find more satisfaction in a shoe than in a cuddly teddy-bear or a doll. They would sometimes pull off the shoes of other children and carry them about or push them up and down, like toy cars, on the floor or on the seat of a chair. One can understand why a shoe may be a very interesting plaything for a child living in a very deprived environment: it is an interesting shape, it has a smell, it is easy to hold and drag or push along, it can be swung by its laces, it sometimes has a shining buckle on it, it is nice to push one's hands into, and it can be enjoyably sucked. Another advantage is that it is linked to people, *i.e.* it has to be pulled from another child's foot, which often elicits some kicks or shouts from that child, and it may also promote adult attention if a member of staff comes over and takes the shoe. Some of the children spent a lot of time pulling off other children's shoes and getting grumbled at by the staff for doing so.

Wheelchairs were another popular plaything with the mobile children; they would turn over a wheelchair and sit spinning its wheels, or would crawl about pushing an empty wheelchair in front of them, or take out its cushions and throw them about.

Understanding play

Part of the problem of play in the wards was the lack of understanding about *how* children play, and how mothering and play are inseparable. Staff often appeared to find difficulty in appreciating that routine care, such as dressing, washing and bathing, could themselves be an opportunity for mothering the children and playing with them. For example, one evening when 12-year-old Ralph was in the bath, he put his hand over the plug-hole and lifted it up and down, releasing a little water at a time and smiling as he controlled the noisy gurgles of the down-flowing water. Ralph was blind but had good hand ability. The student who had just finished bathing him and was about to lift him out of the bath became very anxious when he did this, and said "No, no, that is mischief". She did not appreciate that Ralph was enjoying the feeling and noise of the water as it gushed away, and enjoying his control of it: she believed his behaviour was naughty because it was 'time-wasting'. The simplicity of bathtime play as a form of learning and mothering had not been explained to this young student.

RECOMMENDATIONS

This chapter shows that the children in long-stay hospitals are deprived of mothering and play to an appalling degree. Two major issues related to mothering care emerge from this chapter. Firstly, does institutionalisation *have* to result in multiply handicapped children losing, or never developing, the ability to obtain staff attention? And is this due to the fact that the present organisation of institutional care prevents staff and children interacting with each other, eventually resulting in both children and staff developing deep-seated habits of non-involvement (*i.e.* the ignored child no longer looks for mothering attention from staff, and the nurses cease to think that the child needs that attention)? Secondly, if the present organisation of hospitals *is* causing staff to develop habits of non-involvement with the children, then what may be the best way in which to help them have better insight into the fact that handicapped children in institutions are especially vulnerable to deprivation of mothering care?

The following recommendations might be helpful in forming the basis of guidelines to ease the children's deprivation.

(1) There should be continuity of staff, *i.e.* a definite ruling against constant changes of staff in children's wards (see also recommendation 5, p. 98).

(2) If some members of ward staff make a relationship with a child it should be respected and encouraged, and not derided as 'spoiling' the child.

(3) If a child has a special member of staff who is off duty, other staff should be aware of any small personal routine which the child and that member of staff have developed, and it should be maintained in order to give the child some security (see special example, p. 108).

(4) Staff should be aware that certain groups of children are especially vulnerable to lack of attention; for example blind, non-ambulant children (see pp. 115-116).

(5) Staff should be aware that their own need to get feed-back from the children may lead them to give an unwise quality of attention to certain more

able children in the group, which may not be very helpful to those children (see pp. 117 and 118).

(6) Furniture should not 'imprison'. Furnishings should not be bought solely in order to improve the appearance of the ward but rather with the purpose of making social interaction easier. Care should be taken not to isolate the children for many hours in bean-bags, wheelchairs and armchairs; they should be grouped in clusters instead of in rows, and be within touching distance of each other and adults. Their positions should be changed frequently and they should have some periods free on the floor, when they might be encouraged to romp together (see p. 121-123).

(7) Toys should be purchased with the aim of helping the children to interact with each other and the staff, rather than merely to decorate the ward.

(8) Staff meetings on the *development and maintenance of good child care practices* should be regularly held. (The production of this report necessitated spending 18 months in hospitals, but never during that time was there any evidence of hospital staff meeting to discuss principles of child care in relation to the residential care of handicapped children.)

(9) All staff working with children in long-stay hospitals should be given some insight into child development, the effects of institutional care, and the children's play and mothering needs. This could be done through lectures, discussion groups, films, visits to other centres for handicapped and non-handicapped children (day centres, playgroups, residential homes and schools), recommended reading, and demonstrations of good practice.

CHAPTER 8

Conclusions: The Reality of the Situation and What is Needed

The situation for the nurses was described in Chapter 6, in which the main thesis was that ward nurses were in an unhappy position because of staff shortages, a lack of continuity of staff and a scarcity of supporting services. The unenviable position of the majority of ward nurses seems to be largely responsible for the scenes of deprivation described in Chapter 7, in which the main point of concern was that the children's development and behaviour were being adversely affected because they were so severely deprived of mothering care. One of the major reasons for the children's deprivation is that there has never been any local or national policy for safeguarding the interests of children in long-stay hospitals. Neither the Department of Health and Social Security nor the Department of Education and Science, the two large government departments with legislative powers to help children, have laid down a policy of child care for children living in long-stay hospitals.

Although this study has been concerned specifically with the care of children living in the special-care wards of mental handicap hospitals, the findings and recommendations are relevant to any child who is mentally or physically handicapped, or both, and who is living in any type of long-stay hospital. There are approximately 5000 children living permanently in mental handicap hospitals, some in special-care wards and others in ambulant wards. There are another 1500 children living in other types of long-stay hospitals (children's hospitals, small units attached to geriatric or orthopaedic hospitals, ex-fever or ex-tuberculosis hospitals) who are not classed as being mentally handicapped. The majority of the 1500 are physically disabled and of average or above-average intelligence, although a proportion have some degree of mental handicap in addition to their physical disability. The discussion and suggestions in the following pages apply to all these 6500 children.

It is often assumed that all the children are living in long-stay hospitals in order to receive medical care. However, this study shows (especially in Chapter 3) how even children with grave multiple disabilities rarely get the medical services which they are assumed to be in hospital for. Nor do they get the family-style care which, as children living permanently away from their own homes, they are entitled to receive according to the recommendations of the Curtis Report of 1946 and the subsequent Children Act of 1948 (the Report and Act from which all policies of residential child-care have since developed, but which have not yet benefited children in long-stay hospitals). The main reason why children in long-stay hospitals have not benefited from the new legislation over the last 30 years, intended to protect children in residential care, is that their 'homes' (the long-stay hospitals) are still run on the traditional lines of institutions rather than as substitute homes. Thus, as has been shown in this study, children in long-stay hospitals continue to receive institutional care similar to the standard of care received in the large orphanages of pre-Curtis Report days, and they have no spokesman to ensure that the necessary changes are made. For example, social workers take no responsibility for ensuring that children in long-stay hospitals receive the same standard of care as those in residential homes or institutions run by local authorities (see pp. 30-31).

The lack of strong guidance from the Department of Health and Social Security on the development of good practices of child care in long-stay hospitals permits the children's deprivation to continue unabated, and largely unchallenged. Patterns of care are dictated by rules which are necessary for the efficient running of a large institution, rather than by the individual needs of growing children. For example, this study describes evening activities being restricted because of the need to hand over a tidy ward to night staff; children being sat at tables to wait for their lunch at 11.20 because the central kitchen might send the meal to the ward as early as 11.30; children being put into night-wear as early as 5pm because hours of duty deplete numbers of ward staff by 6pm; and children sitting alone for many hours because the staff have to sort laundry or do other domestic work.

In many hospitals efforts are being made to improve the children's lives by purchasing new furniture and toys and by building playrooms onto the wards, but as this study shows, material improvements are not being matched by an increase in numbers of staff who have the insight to give the children individual care and make wise use of the better facilities.

At present, if hospital staff of any discipline are asked about their hospital's child-care practices, they usually make vague references to "the need to provide a domestic setting for the children", and they describe how the wards have been "up-graded" by the purchase of toys, personal clothing, the partitioning of wards into cubicles, the provision of colourful curtains, counterpanes, lockers, mobiles and murals. These answers indicate a lack of insight into the fact that good practices in child care cannot be achieved solely by material improvements. Hospital staff should be more aware of the human element in residential care; for example the prevention of childhood loneliness, continuity of staff, the children's need for mothering and play, the importance of helping children to stretch out their hands, and the need to give the children opportunities to develop as individuals capable of making secure relationships with each other and with staff, despite their grave handicaps.

The main conclusion to be drawn from this study is that it is time for a definite *child care policy* to be spelled out for long-stay hospitals, which would be *easily applicable at ward level*, although being initially defined by the

Department of Health and Social Security. Such a policy would cover two major needs.

(1) The first need is the appointment, in every Regional Health Authority, of two 'inspector/co-ordinators' of services for all children in long-stay hospitals (with 14 Regional Health Authorities this would mean a total of only 28 appointments). These people would be responsible for co-ordinating and supervising the *whole care* of children living in long-stay hospitals, for example his receipt of medical and paramedical services, his education, his quality of mothering care, his family contact, and in-service training for his staff. They would have direct knowledge of handicapped children, knowledge of normal child development, be fully aware of principles of good residential care for children, and be familiar with all the local centres, schools and other facilities for handicapped children. They would also be in close contact with the regional branches of all the voluntary organisations concerned with handicapped children. These inspectors essentially would be *spokesmen* for the children in long-stay hospitals. They must not be officers or managers of the local health or social services who are merely assuming part-time responsibility for long-stay hospital children as an additional duty, but should be full-time, separately appointed people who are professionally independent of local issues and services, and responsible directly to the Secretary of State rather than to the Area Management Team of the Area Health Authority in whose hospitals the children live. However, they would work in close collaboration with the district Handicap Teams (see Appendix 2 on the Court Committee proposals). They would also be in close touch with the Children's Team of the Health Advisory Service when it is visiting the area.

(2) The second need is the drawing-up of practical guidelines on daily care of children in long-stay hospitals. These guidelines would be of prime importance in improving standards of child care, and part of the work of the regional inspector/co-ordinators would be to ensure that these guidelines are adhered to. Chapters 2 to 7 of this study contain advice and recommendations which might form the basis of such guidelines; for example on maintaining family contact, the rôle of hospital teachers, social workers and therapists, the use of volunteers, the need for continuity of staff in children's wards, and the need to give more professional support to nurses at ward level.

The finance of change

The suggestion that inspector/co-ordinators should be appointed in every Regional Health Authority would involve considerable expense, perhaps £120,000 to £150,000 per year in salaries alone (from central government) for the total of 28 new appointments. Increases in ward staff and therapy staff would also put unwelcome financial pressures on Regional Health Authorities, especially those regions in which there are a number of long-stay hospitals. However, many of the recommendations which have been made throughout this report would cost very little to implement: for example it does not cost anything to place a non-ambulant child in such a position in his ward that he may more easily see adult and child activities.

Quite radical changes in ward routines might be considered which would improve the children's quality of care, but not necessitate massive financial expenditure. For example, one idea might be to blur the edges between the school day and the ward day by letting the children go to school from 10.30am until 2.30pm and let them have lunch afterwards. This would allow a more relaxed getting-up period and a leisurely breakfast, followed by a long period in school without the harassment of going back to the ward (perhaps a milk-and-biscuit break could be had in school at noon), and then the children could have a relaxed lunch back in the ward at 2.30. This would leave a period for evening play, therapy and outings, and supper could be given slowly at 6.30, followed by bed at 7.30 to 8.30, with the night staff doing the tidying-up of the day-time activities. Such a day would be very different from the present organisation of the children's day. It would mean changes in staff hours, and would also affect the catering staff who prepare the meals and the domestic staff who clean up after them. However, unless radical and imaginative changes are tried in an attempt to break away from institutional organisation, the children will continue to be mere units in a system of fragmented care which causes them to be alternately harassed for short periods and ignored for long periods, and gives little satisfaction to the staff who work with them.

Staff training

There are theories that a different form of staff training (*i.e.* 'care staff' training instead of nursing training) will prevent the deprivation suffered by children in long-stay hospitals. A DHSS committee, under the chairmanship of Mrs. Peggy Jay, is at present preparing a report on the training of staff working with mentally handicapped people, and it is possible that this will draw attention to the need for special training for staff who work with mentally handicapped children in residential care. However, there is no guarantee that changes in training will substantially improve the quality of care being given to children in long-stay hospitals. Advocates of a changed form of training as a means of helping the children may be underestimating the fact that the organisational rules of a large institution exert a powerful influence on staff behaviour, regardless of their type of training. (It is significant that a Sister I met in this study, who had an SCN certificate and an NNEB certificate, as well as being an RNMS, and who had also worked in children's Homes, still organised her ward in the same manner as those sisters whose training and experience had been only in mental handicap hospitals. The children in her ward were bathed and toileted *en masse*, were prepared early for bed, and had few play activities.) It must also be remembered that, regardless of whether the staff originally train as nurses or as residential-care staff, there will always be a risk of their becoming professionally depressed and ineffective when they work for years in under-staffed and under-privileged institutions (see pp. 81-84).

From the observations in this study, it would appear that any proposed

132

changes in training, although welcome, may be ineffective unless they are also backed up by massive changes in the hierarchical organisation and the philosophy of the institution itself. Reference to training inevitably leads one once again to question the whole concept of the large institution as a form of permanent care for handicapped children. Perhaps all children's wards in long-stay hospitals should be made completely independent of the rest of the hospital and become the administrative responsibility of either:

(a) the local education authorities (being regarded as special boarding-schools with all staff employed by the local education authority, the care of the children being the responsibility of the head teacher, teachers and care staff, and the teachers doing extraneous duties as they do in boarding schools); or
(b) the local authority social service departments (being regarded as children's Homes, with care staff employed by the local authority and the children going out to special schools in the community).

Either of the above solutions should be clearly recognised as only a *temporary measure* to try to improve the quality of life for children at present in long-stay hospitals. It would be a grave mistake if either solution were adopted and then retained permanently as a development of hospital-type accommodation under another name: if this happened it could encourage the admission of handicapped children to long-stay hospitals and so discourage the development of accommodation in the local community. To prevent this happening, it would be necessary for a clear statement to be issued emphasizing that the changes were *temporary*, to help children *at present* in long-stay hospitals, and were *not* intended to replace community care.

It is relevant here to point out that in some mental handicap hospitals in various parts of the country, small groups of the more able children have been taken out of the children's wards and accommodated in what had been staff houses in the grounds of the hospitals. The nurses who care for the children in these houses have been given a certain independence with regard to the children's meals, holidays and daily lives, and the change seems to have resulted in a better standard of child care and much happier nurses. In view of this, it would seem wise for any report on a proposed new form of training to include strong recommendations that children's wards should be administered as autonomous homes, staffed by permanent care-staff who are independent of the hospital organisation. Such a recommendation would be one way of using any newly trained staff together with long-established nursing staff, until such a time as large mental handicap institutions and other long-stay hospitals are closed altogether, and all handicapped children are accommodated in small homes or foster-homes in the local community.

As to the therapy needed by physically handicapped children, it would be most helpful if this could be given by the staff who have most contact with the children, that is as a 24-hour 'way of life' for the children rather than as something that is 'done to' them for short periods on premises away from their wards. Therefore it seems necessary that the training syllabus of staff to work with handicapped children — whether they follow a nursing training or some

133

new form of care-staff training — should include physiotherapy, speech therapy and occupational therapy, so that the new staff can assume an informed and responsible rôle in the child's therapy. This proposal may be seen by therapists as a threat to their profession; however, if care staff (or nurses) do have a definite rôle as therapists it could be regarded more as an advantage to the children than as a threat to a profession which is unable to offer much help to the children because few therapists are willing to work in long-stay hospitals.

Integration

The idea of integrating handicapped children into groups of non-handicapped children is the subject of much discussion. However, it would seem from the selection/rejection procedures now being commonly practised in many special schools that people who are actually working with handicapped children are some of the strongest opponents of integration. For example schools for the blind will reject physically handicapped blind children; schools for the deaf will exclude mentally handicapped deaf children; schools for physically handicapped children will exclude physically handicapped children who are also deaf and mentally handicapped; and most special schools will try to pass on children who have very difficult behaviour problems. Some people working with handicapped children subscribe to the idea of 'pure' handicaps, *i.e.* 'the deaf', 'the blind', 'the physically disabled', and they want children to fall into one easily definable single category of handicap. This is often the reason why children with complicated multiple handicaps end up in long-stay hospitals.

While many people would agree that to put a lot of multiply handicapped children together in wards such as have been described in this study is to create ghettos which are good for neither children nor staff, those same people might also maintain that such children cannot be accepted into groups of more able children. I would question this latter idea. Before working on this report, I was employed in a children's long-stay hospital which had a mental handicap department and a paediatric department, and my experience there was that it *was* possible to successfully mix multiply handicapped children who had widely varying intellectual abilities. The children I worked with were all physically disabled and non-ambulant, although some could crawl; some were above average in intelligence, others were mildly mentally handicapped, and a few were very severely so. The reasons why these children mixed together very well were probably that: (*a*) the group was small, generally not more than 10 children; (*b*) the severely mentally handicapped children were in the minority, generally not more than three in the group at any one time; (*c*) the most severely handicapped children were always 'given a place' in the group, that is they were included in all activities, outings, clubs, holidays; (*d*) the more intelligent children were encouraged to have positive attitudes to the most severely handicapped members of the group, and to recognise that they could contribute to such group activities as painting, cooking, dressing-up, or drama; and (*e*) staff knew that the most handicapped children should always be regarded as full members of the group, and should not be left out of activities or put at a disadvantage because of their extreme helplessness.

Since 1972, Dr. Barnardo's organisation has been integrating mentally handicapped children into three homes for non-handicapped children in the north-west of England. Alan Kendall, Divisional Director, (Child Care) of Dr. Barnardo's N.W. Division, has described the scheme[15]. Some of the children had multiple physical disabilities, in addition to varying degrees of mental handicap, but they were not excluded from the scheme. Alan Kendall stated:

"Problems there are, but given the commitment, sufficient numbers of staff, their good-will and a bit of imagination, it is our experience that most problems can be adequately dealt with. The problems presented by mentally handicapped children have been found to be common among non-handicapped children — and this point cannot be over-emphasised . . ."
and

"As with the staff, so the non-handicapped children also need preparation before any integration can take place. They need careful explanation in language they can understand and also a clear role to play in helping the handicapped children . . ."

Dr. Barnardo's is working similar schemes of integration in other areas too. If such schemes were repeated in all voluntary society children's homes and in all local authority homes, the numbers of children now living in long-stay mental handicap hospitals and other types of long-stay hospitals could be drastically reduced.

15. Kendall, A. (1973) 'Integrated residential services for mentally handicapped and non-handicapped children.' Paper presented at Third International Congress of the International Association for the Scientific Study of Mental Deficiency, The Hague.

Scenes in Ward 7

Ward 7 accommodated 21 multiply handicapped children aged from three to 14 years. 18 of the children were receiving permanent long-term care, two were weekly boarders, and one was in for short-term care. Nine of the 18 long-term children had been admitted for permanent care before the age of five years.

Thirteen of the 21 children were non-ambulant, 19 were incontinent, four were known to be blind, 19 were speechless. 20 did not wash or dress themselves and seven did not feed themselves. All had the ability to grasp objects in their hands.

All the problems which have been discussed in this report were found to be incorporated in Ward 7, and this appendix describes some typical scenes in the ward. The overriding impression of the ward was the intense alone-ness of the children who lived in it.

A typical evening

At 4pm

Two of the 21 children had been taken home for the night, and one was out with his foster-mother. Nursing Assistant Jones, and State Enrolled Nurse Smith were on duty for the remaining 18 children. There was a new little girl in the ward today: six-year-old Mary. She was ambulant, and had been admitted to the 'sick' ward a week ago for short-term care, and had just been transferred to Ward 7. She stood in the middle of the day-room, cuddling a soft toy hippo which she had brought from home, and looking timidly about her.

The day-room contained a battered settee, a large air-bed, and some wooden boxes with holes in and square boxes arranged as three steps. Ambulant children were walking about; the non-ambulant children were lying on the floor. A few children sat under the radiators and held the warm pipes with their hands, others rested their bare feet on the pipes. There was a sense of poverty in the room, and it was slightly cold.

A narrow corridor led from the day-room, on each side of which were linen cupboards, store-rooms, a bathroom, washroom and lavatories. The corridor led into the bedroom, which was so small that the beds were in rows across the centre of the room as well as all around the sides. The children's clothes were kept in two large cupboards just inside the bedroom. There was no room for individual lockers. The day-room had a newly-built extension to it, known as 'the sun-lounge'. At one end of this sun-lounge there was a colour television, a plastic settee, three plastic armchairs and a strip of carpet. At the other end there was a sideboard minus its doors, four tables, and ten kitchen-type chairs; this was where the children ate their meals.

At 4.15

Supper started. There was a shortage of clean bibs, so soiled ones were reused. These dirty bibs were lying in a damp heap in the broken-doored sideboard, and as the staff lifted them out a sour smell of stale food arose, and lumps of cold porridge, potato and sponge-pudding fell from them. They were shaken and then tied around the children's necks. There was also a shortage of bowls and spoons, which caused a major inconvenience during supper because the two staff had to keep leaving the children and running to the kitchen to rinse bowls and spoons. When they did this, some of the more able children went to the trolley and ate scraps from the scrap bowl, or grabbed food from the plates of the less able children. As it was so inconvenient to keep going to the kitchen to wash dishes in the middle of feeding the children, the staff eventually gave some of the children their puddings in unwashed bowls which had been used by other children.

Fourteen of the children could feed themselves, which was said to be due to the psychologists of the hospital directing the ward staff in the principles of behaviour modification. The ability to feed themselves appeared to be an isolated skill, for only two of the 14 children were also reliable about the lavatory, and only one of them could wash and dress himself.

The children were given their meals in two sittings, so that they could be individually supervised. Those who could manage without help were encouraged by praise, and the others were encouraged to lift their spoons to their mouths on their own after being helped to load them. Thus while actually sitting at the table with a plate of food in front of them and spoons in their hands, the children received attention. However, immediately a child finished eating he ceased to receive attention. Some of the non-ambulant children were then carried silently back into the day-room and placed, still sticky, onto bean-bags. Others remained sitting at the tables; their faces were covered with food and they sucked at their food-covered hands. A few of the children got off their chairs as they finished eating and went under the tables, where they used their hands to shovel up spilt food into their mouths. Some of the ambulant and crawling children went to the waste-bowl on the trolley and picked at the slimy mess of everybody else's leavings, and poked into the bowl containing the dirty cutlery to suck off the food which had been left on other children's spoons. Then they went to the slower eaters and tried to take food from them.

At 4.55

The staff cleared the tables, went into the kitchen and remained there to have a cup of tea. Nursing Assistant Hartley arrived at 5pm. She would be on duty until 8pm. She joined the other two staff in the kitchen.

The 18 children were left without supervision. Eight-year-old Monty (two

137

years in hospital) and 14-year-old Douglas (11 years in hospital), both ambulant, began to tip over the chairs in the sun-lounge, and leant on the window-sills and opened and slammed the windows. They were high-spirited and healthy, and this was their usual behaviour after meals. Seven-year-old James (five years in hospital) was sitting in a baby-buggy at the end of the sun-lounge. His buggy got tipped over during the rompings of Monty and Douglas. He was unharmed but very startled. Monty began to loudly slam the low gate between the lounge and the day-room.

Nine-year-old Shirley remained sitting at the table where she had eaten her supper. She was a weekly boarder, and spent most of her time between Monday and Friday sitting at a table in the sun-lounge, in a state of silent, abject misery. She had a frail appearance, and wore a caliper on one leg. She had had a stressful time towards the end of supper today, because her plate had been snatched first by 13-year-old Elizabeth and then by Douglas (who had proceeded to eat her supper with his fingers). Shirley always ate very slowly, and she often had her food stolen by the more able children.

Three-year-old Tom, ambulant, but with very little sight, wandered about the two rooms. Sometimes he sat down on the floor. He had been admitted to the hospital only a few days before, and was in for long-term care. Mary, the new little girl, stood looking through the day-room doors into the corridor. Her toy hippo appeared to be lost. She held her hands limply at her sides.

At 5.30

The children's drugs were given out. This was the first staff involvement with the children since 4.55. The SEN stood in the corridor beside the drug trolley. The two Nursing Assistants stood by her with dessert spoons in their hands. The SEN put the appropriate drug for each child into one of the spoons held by the NAs, who had meanwhile filled the spoons with jam from a pot standing on the drug-trolley. The NA then opened the day-room door, found the right child for the drug, and pushed the spoonful of jam and the capsule into his mouth. (This was the usual procedure for giving drugs in Ward 7: it was done hurriedly and without conversation with the child.) Because so much jam had been put into their mouths the children became very sticky: they continued to sit about with sticky faces and with jam trickling down their chins onto the front of their clothes. Little streaks of dried jam, long there and hardened now, were stuck on the radiator in the day-room because the children on numerous previous drug-giving occasions had wiped their sticky mouths along the radiator by which they had been sitting when given their drugs. There were also streaks of fluff-covered jam down the sides of the wheelchairs.

SEN Smith went off duty at 5.35. NA Hartley and NA Jones would be in charge of the ward for the rest of the evening, and would have to get the 18 children ready for bed, and their clothing sorted out by 8pm. Neither had had any training in looking after handicapped children, or in residential care work. NA Jones was middle-aged and had started working in the hospital 18 months earlier. She said that on her first day she had been given the choice of spending a week looking around the hospital at the various wards, or starting work straight away as an NA on Ward 7. She had decided to begin as a nurse immediately, but had been very upset for a few days because of the children's grave handicaps. She had not attended any lectures or been given any guidance. She said that she "just picked up what to do" from the other staff. She was kind to the children, and with different leadership would have made an excellent houseparent. NA Hartley was in her late twenties and had been working in the hospital for seven months. She said that she had applied to the hospital for domestic work but had been offered a job as a nursing assistant.

5.40 to 7.25

NA Hartley and NA Jones had to be in the bathroom, washroom and bedroom during this period, and a number of children were left unsupervised in the day-room. Non-ambulant children who were waiting their turn to be bathed or washed, or who had already had their turn, were lying on the floor by the radiator or sitting in wheelchairs or baby-buggies. The ambulant children wandered about the day-room and sun-lounge. Douglas and Monty continued to rampage about in the sun-lounge, shoving at the tipped-over chairs. Nine-year-old Dermod (four years in hospital), cerebral-palsied but able to crawl, remained in the corner where he always put himself after meals. He rested his bare feet on the warm pipes.

Shirley still sat alone at the bare table in the sun-lounge, where she had been sitting since finishing her supper at 4.55. She had shrunk into herself as Douglas's romps with the chairs continued unabated around her, and, completely still, she stared blankly at the untidy, comfortless scene in front of her.

Mary began to strip little pieces of wall-paper off the day-room wall. She dropped the paper on the floor. Six-year-old Jill, who had been admitted to the hospital the year before, bottom-shuffled along behind Mary, picked up the bits of wallpaper and ate them.

NA Jones was working in the small bathroom, undressing and washing one child at a time on a large table. NA Hartley was with a group of children in the wash-room/lavatory area. She was following the usual wash-room routine of sitting four or five children on the lavatories and then partially or fully undressing them as they sat there. After sitting on the lavatories for about 10 minutes, each child was taken across to the wash-basins to be washed. If he was non-ambulant, he was lifted onto a large table in front of the lavatories and washed as he lay there.

The children in the washroom were being washed with one shared flannel. There appeared to be a shortage of bathroom commodities; nappies were being used as towels, and there were only two hairbrushes for all the children. All underwear and nightclothes were communal, including the standard issue dressing-gown made of towelling.

Twelve-year-old Brian (in hospital for nine years) had dried mucus caked

139

on his face because his nose had not been wiped for him for many hours. The mucus could not be removed, even after being soaked with the flannel. NA Hartley decided to leave it on in case his face was made sore by too much rubbing. Brian was a very big boy, and it was difficult to find pyjamas to fit him. The jacket eventually put on him was too tight and came high up his back.

Some of the children were returned to the day-room after being put into nightclothes. They were not wearing slippers, and their feet were cold.

Although the two NAs were almost overwhelmed by their chores, they were very kind to the children during the getting-to-bed routines. NA Jones called me into the bathroom to see a child smiling as she washed him, and she took me to see children whom she had put to bed. She went to each bed and peeped at the children. She said: "It makes you wonder, doesn't it? I wish there was more time to spend with them and play with them as we would our own".

At 7pm the washing and changing of children was all finished. Eight children were in bed; 10 were back in the day-room, dressed in their nightclothes. It had taken the two NAs 1 hour 20 minutes to attend to the 18 children. The NAs began to tidy up the bathroom and washroom, and pack up the dirty clothes. The 10 children in the day-room were in the following positions:
10-year-old June sat in a wheelchair, sucking her hands;
nine-year-old Dermod was in the corner where he was always to be found; he was stripping off his nightwear;
six-year-old Jill was shuffling around the room on her bottom;
13-year-old Elizabeth sat beside Brian on the air-bed, on which eight-year-old Monty lay asleep;
six-year-old Mary walked wearily up and down the room;
13-year-old Charles, blind, stood holding the radiator;
14-year-old Douglas was kneeling in the middle of the day-room floor;
three-year-old Tom stood holding the radiator.

At 7.25

The two NAs had just finished packing the laundry. They walked through the day-room into the sun-lounge, turned on the colour television and put Jill in front of it. Then they went into the kitchen, where they sat smoking and drinking coffee. While it seemed wrong that the children were left alone so much, these two women must have been very hot and tired because they had washed and changed 18 children since 5.40pm and had tidied up the bathroom and packed up all the dirty laundry.

At 7.30 the positions of the children were:
June was in her wheelchair, as before.
Dermod was still in his corner, now stripped, and he lay on his back playing with a wheelchair tray that had been on the floor near him. He held it onto his face and twiddled with the rods and screws.
Jill was crouched in front of the television in the sun-lounge.

Elizabeth, Brian and Monty were still on the air-bed.

Mary stood in the middle of the room, now sucking her hands.

Charles had sat down on the floor, his back against the radiator, and his hands and arms stretched out each side of the warm pipes. He looked very cold.

Douglas was still kneeling in the middle of the floor.

Tom still stood by the radiator.

At 8pm the staff were still in the kitchen and the 10 children were in the same positions as before.

One afternoon, for four children

Again, the ward was under-staffed, and from 1pm until 4.30pm the staff were not involved with the children at all. During these hours the staff were in the bedroom, day-room or kitchen.

At 1pm, 12-year-old Percy (six years in hospital), partially sighted, cerebral-palsied and non-ambulant, was in a wheelchair. The chair did not have a foot-rest, and Percy's feet were dangling just above a narrow metal bar. At 1.15, 13-year-old Elizabeth crawled across to Percy and removed his socks. He continued to sit in the chair, bare-footed, until he was taken to the table for his supper at 4.30. By that time his bare feet had been hovering just above the metal bar of his broken wheelchair for 3 hours 15 minutes. His feet looked thin, cold and frail, and appeared to need some warm support, such as a cushion, to be placed under them.

At 1pm, eight-year-old Hector (four years in hospital, cerebral-palsied and non-ambulant) was lying on his back in a bean-bag in a very awkward position. He remained in that position until lifted for supper at 4.30.

At 1pm, 13-year-old Angela (nine years in hospital) was in her wheelchair in the sun-lounge, when she began crying. She cried unheeded until 4pm, and then became quiet. She was put to the table for supper at 4.30.

At 2pm, six-year-old Jill (one year in hospital) became very miserable at seeing two mothers and a father come to visit other children. She crouched at the door of the day-room, weeping and moaning, for 20 minutes. Then she resumed her usual behaviour of bottom-shuffling about the day-room, endeavouring to get staff attention. When the staff were in the bathroom or bedroom, Jill sat by the day-room door and tried to prise it open by curling the fingers of her 'good' hand under it, hoping to open it and get through to the staff. Whenever the staff came through the door they inevitably bumped into Jill as she crouched by the door. This appeared to irritate them, especially when she also tried to catch hold of their feet as they entered. She was not a popular child. Eventually the staff placed Jill on the air-bed, where she was anchored for some 15 minutes before managing to crawl off and once more resume her place at the day-room door.

The loneliness of three-year-old Tom

Tom had just been admitted to Ward 7. He knew the hospital through coming in for occasional day-care, but this was his first experience of residential care. He was ambulant, frail-looking, and described as "almost blind". The staff thought that he would remain permanently in the hospital because his family had complicated housing, financial and health problems.

Saturday afternoon, a few days after Tom's admission

From 1pm to 3pm there were 16 children and four staff in the ward. Ambulant children were wandering aimlessly about; non-ambulant children lay on the floor or sat in wheelchairs. Tom walked up and down, his head on one side. Sometimes he stood motionless in the middle of the room, or by the window. Sometimes he stood tapping his mouth with his hands. Several times he went and pulled at the curtains. Once he twirled himself up in a curtain, standing under it and folding it around him, and then whirling round and round on the spot until the curtain enfolded him like a cocoon. He unwound himself, then lay beneath the curtain and held it in one hand, and moved his body round and round in a small circle by pushing and tapping on the floor with one foot. A passing member of staff said "I think he might be blind and deaf". Tom received no attention from anyone during this two-hour period.

A few days later: mid-morning

There were again four staff on duty. Tom had been standing holding the radiator for some 10 minutes, then he moved away and walked across the room. He did not see nine-year-old Dermod lying on the floor, and almost trod on Dermod's face. Tom stumbled, bent down, felt at Dermod with both hands, stumbled again, and then pulled gently at Dermod's clothes. Dermod, partially sighted, pushed gently back at Tom. Tom swayed back and sat down hard on the floor. He remained sitting, felt all around him with one hand, bottom-shuffled around Dermod, felt his way to the wall, and then stood up. He then walked to the middle of the room and stood there tapping his mouth with one hand.

This episode, with staff guidance, might have been a valuable opportunity for the two little boys to learn more about each other. But Tom and Dermod had coped with the situation alone and come through it in muddled isolation. Not being taught to identify themselves and each other, these two poor-sighted children were developing into solitary beings without any meaningful experience of communicating with other people. Of course it is common for three-year-olds to be unsociable, but the organisation of Ward 7 encouraged the staff to develop habits of non-involvement with the children, and was likely to keep Tom at this solitary stage in his development. No attempts were being made to encourage social interaction between the children in Ward 7, not even in such primary ways as feeling each other's hands, and finding pleasure and recognition in touching each other and hearing their own and each other's names.

142

Later that morning Tom had his first bit of mothering. As the staff brought the lunch-trolley into the day-room, he fell over and began to cry. He cried for four minutes, then a nurse picked him up and cuddled him for one minute. He stopped crying. When the nurse put him down he immediately resumed his crying, whereupon another nurse picked him up. He stopped crying again. She held him for a moment, then went to put him down. He wound his legs around her thighs and knees, slipping to her calves and feet as she struggled to lower him to the ground and let go of him again. He would not easily be put down, he clung to her and his cries and protests increased in volume. "I don't like to put him down", the young nurse said as she finally managed to extricate herself from his entwining legs and arms. She walked away. Tom remained in a heap in the middle of the floor, weeping. Such a situation, caused by the organisation (*i.e.* lunch was about to start) not only teaches a young child about rejection; it also teaches a young nurse how to steel herself, *against her better judgement*, to ignore a child's appeals for mothering.

Throughout the afternoon Tom wandered about the room, wound himself up in the curtain, or just stood sucking his thumb. In mid-afternoon a member of the staff took him for a 20-minute walk in a baby-buggy around the hospital grounds. When he came back he was placed in the day-room and the staff went into the kitchen for their tea. Tom then went to the curtain and again began to wind himself up in it.

That evening: 5.45

Tom was looking very distressed and tired. His day had been lonely and wearisome. I had been in the ward since 9am and had not seen him receive any direction to his activities, nor any rest or security. Like Mary, the other new child in the ward, he had spent the day walking about the day-room and sun-lounge. The staff had not settled him into a spot which he might have felt was his own, perhaps giving him a small chair and a table of his own with familiar toys on it, the company of nearby children, and cuddles from the staff, all of which might have helped to reassure him as a young handicapped child away from home for the first time.

He came to where I was sitting and seemed to want comforting, but he pulled away as I drew him to me. Suddenly he began to rush about and rattle wheelchairs, in a burst of anger. He hurled himself at seven-year-old James' buggy and shook it, then shook Percy's wooden chair, then went to 13-year-old Angela and punched her knees and legs, but his small fists did not seem to disturb Angela. He then rushed back to me and burrowed into my lap. His sleeves were wet where he had been sucking them, and he looked flushed and exhausted.

The three nurses who were on duty came across and looked at Tom. They said that he had only started to suck his sleeves since he had been living in the ward full-time for the last week or so, and they thought he probably copied the habit from other children. Several of the children in Ward 7 had a habit of drawing their jersey sleeves down over their hands and then sucking the material and their hands at the same time. This meant that they often had long damp sleeves hanging down over their hands. Tom had not picked up this habit when he had been coming to the ward for day-care only, but had started doing it about a week after becoming residential. It would seem that such habits are likely to develop when a child has prolonged periods of family deprivation and lack of attention, and when he spends many hours witnessing the long-established institutional habits of other deprived children.

At 7pm

Tom was put into his pyjamas and returned to the day-room to continue his wanderings. Just before 8pm he came again to me and sat in my lap. When I left at 8.15 he did not want me to put him down. He clung around my knees and feet. When I finally managed to get out and shut the ward door I could hear him hammering with his fists on the other side of it, and crying.

A few days later: 5pm

There were 20 children in the ward, with three staff. The staff had just finished giving the children their supper, and were now in the kitchen having their coffee. I heard Tom crying in the sun-lounge and went to see what was happening. He was being hurt by six-year-old Jill, who was holding him down, pressing on his face and pinching him. He had no trousers, pants or nappy on, and he looked dishevelled and tired. I picked him up and took him to the day-room. He was so upset that he broke away, tore across the room in anger, punched Angela (who looked very surprised), and then ran crying into the sun-lounge again, where he flung himself against a radiator and sobbed.

Tom appeared to be in a grave state of homesickness and grief, and seemed to be getting more disturbed each day. It was noticeable that he had deteriorated emotionally during the two weeks since his admission. He was panicky, cried more, sucked his sleeves, got angry and hit out at other children. It was disquieting that the doctors had only that same day said "that child *has* settled in well".

The same evening: 7pm

The staff were in the bathroom, changing children. Tom stood in the middle of the day-room. He was bare-footed and dressed in hospital pyjamas which were too big for him. The floor was wet because the domestic worker had just washed it. When Tom moved forward his bare feet slipped on the wet floor; he sat down and began to cry. Then he got himself up again. The day-room door opened and one of the staff put six-year-old Mary into the room, and just at that point Tom slipped over again on the wet floor. He got up and ran crying to Mary, who was probably the nearest person he could see with his meagre sight. Mary stood bare-footed in her nightie, and Tom clasped her round the waist and tried to climb into her arms. Mary was startled and stepped quickly back; she swayed and nearly fell. The nurse took the weeping

144

Tom away from Mary and put him to one side, then she went back to the bathroom.

Mary's loneliness

Within a few days of six-year-old Mary being admitted to Ward 7 she had settled into a bleak pattern of behaviour, which consisted mainly of standing about and occasionally stripping tiny pieces of wall-paper off the walls. Or if she could find a newspaper or magazine she would tear it up into tiny scraps and drop them on the floor.

One Sunday

At 12.55 all the children except Mary had finished their lunches and the staff took away the trolley and the dirty dishes. I remained to feed Mary. As she ate her pudding, she kept looking fearfully around at the noisy but harmless rampagings of Nigel and Monty and Douglas. The always-hungry Charles, 13 years old, blind, ambulant and very tall, was attracted by the smell of food still in the room, and he joined the other three boys who were now making efforts to get at Mary's pudding. Nigel, minus his pants, climbed on to the table and sat beside her plate. A member of staff came into the room and saw him sitting bare-bottomed beside Mary's plate: she shouted "get off", but Nigel did not move and the nurse went out again.

Throughout that early afternoon Mary wandered about, tearing up pieces of paper. Nigel had earlier found a magazine and ripped it up: Mary walked around picking up the larger pieces, tearing them up smaller and smaller and scattering the bits around her as she moved. By 2.45 the day-room floor was covered in torn paper as small as confetti.

At 3.30 Mary was still tearing up paper. There were now two nursing assistants and a pupil nurse on duty. They were in the bedroom, sorting out clothes.

At 4pm the staff came into the day-room and exclaimed at the amount of paper on the floor. Mary had been steadily ripping up paper all afternoon.

After tea at 4.55, Mary walked up and down the ward again until she was taken and put into her nightie at 6.25. Then she was returned to the day-room and spent the rest of the evening walking about until she was put to bed at 8.15.

The following day: after supper

Mary continued her desultory wanderings. At 5.15 her tights had slipped down round her knees, her bottom was dirty, and she was rather smelly. She climbed on to one of the large wooden boxes in the corner of the dayroom. The box had a hole in the middle of it, into which Mary slipped as if going down a manhole. I lifted her out; she was crying and frightened.

Nobody had been assigned to ease Mary over her homesickness on admission to the hospital. Like Tom, the other new child, she walked about all day and had no place to call her own. She was simply having to make out on

145

her own, as all the other children had to, and after just under a week in Ward 7 she had become as waif-like as the other children. Her personal belongings had not been cared for: earlier that afternoon the hippo toy which she had brought from home was being chewed by Monty. Mary was learning to live in solitary fashion among a crowd of children who had no contact with each other, and she was cared for by staff who had minimal involvement with the children.

Children with 'territory'

The references to Tom and Mary draw attention to the fact that they had no places of their own in the ward. Their continuous wanderings gave them an air of being lost or in transit. It seemed that these wanderings are typical of new children, and that having 'territory' is more characteristic of children who have been in hospital for a long time. Several of the children who had been in Ward 7 for many years had their own 'territory', which had not been decided by staff but had apparently evolved among the children themselves. For instance, when one walked into the ward one would always find the same half-dozen long-hospitalised children standing or sitting in the same places along the radiators and warm pipes; Dermod would always be in his special corner, Brian and Elizabeth would always be sitting on the air-bed. The children's positions rarely varied, and when staff had finished attending to a child and placed the child back just inside the day-room door, he or she would then crawl, bottom-shuffle or walk to his special place, where he would remain until it was once more time for washing, feeding or changing.

If ever I took Roger or Dermod away from their territory and gave them a cuddle, they would return to the same places as soon as I put them down again. Roger was 11 years old and had been in the hospital for four years. He was blind and cerebral-palsied. Only once did I see him voluntarily move from his territory by the hot pipes: this was when a workman came to the ward and began to burn the paint off the door. Roger was obviously attracted by the burning smell, and he left his spot and crawled across the room and sat by the door. The workman picked him up and placed him on the air-bed. Roger eventually managed to get himself off the air-bed, then he returned to his own territory again.

Although it was characteristic for the long-hospitalised children to have their own territory, they did not seem to have any sense of ownership, and they did not guard their territory. For example, if any of the more active children bumped into them and pushed them out of their territory, they just moved a little way off for a while and then resumed their place as soon as they could. Although it was obvious that the children found security in their anchorage, any sense of ownership or a wish to guard it against others would perhaps have been an advanced social reaction for these children, who, by reason of their grave handicaps and long-term institutional care, were essentially solitary and property-less children.

It is important to note that neither the occupying of personal territory by the long-hospitalised children, nor the ceaseless wanderings of the new children, were in any way related to staff involvement. Both patterns of behaviour appeared to be the result of the institutional care which kept staff/child relationships to a minimum and encouraged the children to develop a 'sub-culture' of their own, which was predominantly solitary.

The following observations of Dermod, who had a set pattern of behaviour and his own territory, illustrate the typical solitariness of long-hospitalised children.

Dermod's territory

Nine-year-old Dermod had been in hospital for four years. He was partially sighted, speechless and non-ambulant. He spent most of his time in one particular corner of the room, and whenever one entered the ward one could be sure of finding him there. He would sit or lie there for hours, with his feet and back against the warm pipes. If a wheelchair tray was on the floor near him he would sometimes bounce this up and down on his chest. Occasionally he would strip off his clothes and wave his vest or nappy over his head. After taking him up for feeding or changing, the staff would put him down on the floor again and he would then make his way back to his corner and resume his position against the warm pipes.

The only time Dermod ventured from his corner was when it was very sunny, and this seemed to be motivated by his wish to obtain, with his limited sight, some sensory stimulation from sunlight. One day Dermod was changed and put down on the floor at 9.30am. He went to his corner. At 10.30 he crawled out of the corner and made towards a patch of sunlight on the floor at the other end of the room. When he reached the sun-patch he lay down on his back, pursed his lips and shot out a fine spray of saliva up into the air above his head. He stared at the motes of moisture as they were flung into the sunbeam, and he reached up and caught at the shining drops with his fingers, waggling his hands above his head. He was still doing this at 11.15.

At 11.20 he rolled over, pressed his head into a nearby bean-bag and began to suck his thumb. Six-year-old Jill shuffled over to him. She punched him and pinched his hands and arms. He cried. I moved Jill to the other side of the room, but she shuffled back to Dermod, pulled his hair and tapped a large plastic skittle on his face. He cried again. I took Jill into the sun-lounge; she remained there.

At 11.30 the four staff were still in the bathroom and the bedroom, tidying up and sorting out laundry. The 18 children had now been alone in the day-room and sun-lounge for more than two hours. Dermod started his spittle activity once more. He continued this until lunch-time at 12.30.

At 1pm, after finishing his lunch, Dermod was put down on the floor and he again crawled to the patch of sun. He lay smiling at his fingers waggling in the glistening spittle motes.

At 1.50, a passing nurse put him on to the air-bed.

At 2.35 Dermod managed to get himself off the air-bed. He made his way

147

over to the sun-patch and resumed his spittle play.

At 3.30 he was catching the final beam of the sun. Shooting his spittle finely up into the beam, he still smiled at his fingers waggling in the shining spray that he created.

At 3.35 the sun went in. Dermod immediately stopped his spittle play. He felt about him, found a nappy on the floor and began to wave this above his head.

At 5.15, after supper, Dermod was put down on the floor; he crawled back to his usual corner and lay along the warm pipes. He held a wheelchair tray; he removed the rods and screws from it and then flapped the flat board up and down on his chest. Dermod stayed in his corner until he was taken out of the room and put into pyjamas at 7.15. He was then returned to the day-room and he crawled to his corner and draped himself along the warm pipes. He was still there when I left the ward at 8.15.

Dermod had spent the whole day without other than necessary attention from staff. During the entire period from 9.30am to 8.15pm I did not see him receive any attention except when being fed, washed and changes, and once when he was removed from his sun-patch to the air-bed at 1.50.

He had created his own solitary occupation from his meagre environment. (The description of Evelyn on pages 104-107 showed similar solitary behaviour.) Like Evelyn, Dermod received minimal attention from his ward staff and he sought his own stimulation from what the environment offered him. His perseverative solitary behaviour had no connection with other human-beings, and he made no sign of expecting or seeking human attention. His peculiar behaviour, like that of so many of the children met during this study, might correctly be described as a result of long-term institutional care. However, it is possible that Dermod was not unhappy: the children who showed more obvious signs of unhappiness were those who were newer to the hospital, for example, Jill (one year in the hospital) and Tom and Mary (only a few weeks in hospital). These newer children, not yet totally institutionalised, were still seeking attention and were being constantly disappointed.

How Nigel played

Eight-year-old Nigel, the most able child in Ward 7, was a weekly boarder. He did not attend the school, and spent all his time in roaming about the ward. He could say a few words, such as "tea-time", "good-bye", "go away", "'ere yah" and "'orsey". He spent a lot of time opening and shutting the windows in the sun-lounge and day-room. His behaviour was largely dependent on where the staff were. When the staff were out of sight (in the bathroom or bedroom), he usually occupied himself with opening and shutting windows or spinning the wheels of wheelchairs. But when staff went through the day-room to the kitchen to have tea and a cigarette, Nigel would climb onto the back of the settee, lean across to the serving hatch and stare through at the staff. Occasionally he would stretch his arm through the hatch, snatch the lid off the tea-pot and call out "*tea*-time". Sometimes when he did

148

this the staff got cross with him, chased him down from the settee and shut the hatch door; but usually they responded to him with smiles and half a biscuit, and repeated his catch-phrases back to him. He was the most popular child in the ward, and received more attention than the other children did. However, although the staff liked Nigel, they frequently talked about how 'naughty' he was, and they did not seem to appreciate that he was leading a very confined life in the ward and that much of his very active behaviour was akin to the normal energetic explorings of any small child.

One day Nigel got an orange 'bouncer' from a corner of the ward; he sat on it and bounced with considerable skill through to the sun-lounge. Some of the more physically disabled children smiled as he went past them on this bright orange object. He bounced through the day-room, out of the door, into the corridor and on to the bedroom (where the staff were folding nappies). The staff took the bouncer from him and put it behind a trolley, out of the children's reach. They put Nigel back in the day-room and shut the door.

Nigel walked around the day-room for a few minutes, then tipped over a heavy wheelchair and began to spin its wheels (a common form of play for children in long-stay hospitals). He spun one wheel rapidly, then knelt down and placed his tongue near the spokes; the spokes whirled past his tongue within a fraction of an inch. He had to put out his tongue a long way in order to keep his nose and chin safe from the fast-spinning spokes. He obviously liked this unusual and dangerous way of playing with the wheel. After keeping his tongue near the spokes for eight minutes, he then placed his tongue near the tyre and continued the rapid spinning.

Fourteen-year-old Douglas (11 years in hospital) came over and watched Nigel. Douglas began to spin the other wheel of the chair, but he did not put out his tongue. Nigel took no notice of Douglas beside him. Douglas frequently chose to be near Nigel and copy what he was doing. Examples of such 'parallel play' may sometimes be noticed in long-stay wards, usually taking place amongst the more able and active children and often involving the manipulation of furniture. For example Douglas and Nigel would rush about together, opening and shutting windows or turning over chairs. But they did not make contact with each other as they enjoyed these activities, which suggests that severely handicapped children need the close involvement and guidance of staff if they are to progress through the normal childhood stages from solitary play to parallel play to sociable play. Without guidance, the children's play will remain solitary and perseverative.

Whose responsibility?

Which professionals could be held responsible for the deprived conditions in Ward 7, and the appalling loneliness of these children?

There were no therapists working in the hospital; social workers never visited the ward; the doctors gave no guidance at ward level, apparently because they were engrossed with committee work and with out-patients; the nurses appeared to be fighting a losing battle because of shortages of staff, and their goodwill and kindness was being dissipated by the poor conditions and lack of support.

Fourteen of the children could feed themselves because psychologists had instructed the ward staff in the principles of behaviour modification (see p. 137). It cannot be denied that it is valuable for ward staff to understand the principles of behaviour modification, because they can then appreciate how a child learns and how he may systematically be taught acceptable skills. However, it seems that although much patience had gone into training the children in the physical skill of feeding themselves, the psychologists took no further part in improving the children's environment. It was disquieting to realise that the children's ability to feed themselves was a social skill made almost meaningless because it had no carry-over into the rest of their lives. It was merely a physical performance, and even a misleading one insofar as it was likely to convince people who did not recognise the children's deprivation that the hospital was providing good care — because the children had been taught to feed themselves.

In this same context, one might well ask what use it was to have taught a child to load his spoon with food and lift it to his mouth if he later crawled under the table and licked up other children's dribblings because there were too few staff to give him constant attention. The psychologists could be said to have created a false situation in teaching children a social skill without at the same time taking action about the deprivation which is inherent in under-staffed institutions, and which denies the children the mothering they need and eventually distorts their development. Perhaps the first priority for the psychologists should have been to effect changes in institutional care rather than to teach children how to manage their spoons.

How much responsibility did the hospital school-teachers take for the care of the children in Ward 7? The teachers said that they were well aware of the poor child-care in the ward, but felt unable to do anything about it in case they spoilt the good relationship which existed between the school staff and the hospital staff. Their lack of action prompts the questions of how much will professionals shut their eyes to in the interests of preserving 'good relationships', and when do professional responsibilities towards the children have to take priority over good relationships?

The Court Report in Relation to the Present Study

The Court Report reviews the historical background to the present child-health services, highlights the many deficiencies in today's services, and makes imaginative, radical recommendations for changes to ensure that all children will in future receive the health care they need.

In the introductory chapter, entitled *Surveying the Scene*, the Committee states that child health in this country

". . emerges as a story of contrast and contradictions; much that is commendable and much also which must be unacceptable in a civilised society and yet is either not appreciated as creating an imperative or else ignored by those who should be taking action." (page 20)

Some of the many subjects covered in the report include: services for newborn babies, sick children and handicapped children; adolescent health problems; dental care; services for children who need psychiatric help; nurses in the field of child health; general practitioners; consultant paediatricians; the rôle of social workers in the health services; therapy; the school health services; the rôle of parents in securing the health needs of their children; and the reorganisation of the National Health Service with regard to the child health services.

Throughout the report there are references to the concern felt by the committee members about children in long-stay hospitals. For example:

"Some of the most depressing evidence we have received concerned handicapped children both at home and in hospital." (page 8)

"The plight of some children who spend years in hospitals is especially disturbing." (page 10)

". . we are particularly sensitive to the needs of the 8000 children living in long stay hospitals. The hospital is the only home many of them will ever know. By the end of the century many thousands of children will have completed an entire childhood in a hospital setting." (para. 1:43)

"Difficulty in providing adequate support in the community, including a serious shortage of day care and residential care facilities (the responsibility of social service departments), means that there are still too many mentally and physically handicapped children not needing medical and nursing care in hospital who nevertheless remain for years as long-stay patients for social reasons. Sadly it seems to us from the visits we have made and the well-documented evidence we have received that the variable progress in meeting the special needs of children in hospital has been least satisfactory in this area. We have seen for ourselves how hollow the lives of these children can be. Early to bed, and early to rise, with few toys and little education and nothing to do at weekends, their quality of life and standard of care are all too often subordinate to régimes and staffing dictated by the organisation of a large institution. We have also seen the caring devotion of staff struggling with professional isolation as well as lack of facilities. The primary responsibility lies not with them but with an insensitive society which chooses to ignore the problem." (para. 4:47) "Evidence to the Committee suggests that although some progress has been made in identifying and solving the problems associated with the care of long-stay children in hospital, in many instances progress has been slow or non-existent, and the standard of child care is still low." (para.14:93)

If one considers the Court Committee Report solely from the point of view of how its comments and recommendations might help children in long-stay hospitals, then the following references would appear to be especially relevant to long-stay children.

(1) The Committee pointed out that there was a need for better collaboration between all professionals, and referred to:
". . the failure of the three main services concerned—health, social work and education—to act in concert to meet the needs of children in long-stay hospitals." (para.16:19)
and
". . just as doctors and nurses and therapists must work as a team within the health services, so the health service must work in partnership with education and social services. Many of the children with the most complex problems, and the most severe handicaps will require help from all three services." (para.5:25)

(2) The Committee pointed out that there was a need for social workers in the health services to have a wider knowledge of child care, and referred to:
"Despite the fact that the hospital service has played the major rôle in the development of paediatrics, and had a greater share of resources in money and staff compared with the community services, there are still many areas where the special needs of children are not recognised in the actual provision of hospital services. It is important here to recognise the contribution that social services can make in the sphere of social understanding of children's needs. The extent to which these social needs have not been met may, to some extent at least, reflect the shortage of social workers with a knowledge of child care working in the hospital services." (para.4:41)
"We would hope that the Social Services department and the social workers in hospital would increasingly concern themselves with the wider social issues involved in caring for children in hospital, and that the experience gained in the field of residential child care would be drawn upon." (para.18:72)

"The hospital-based social worker has an important part to play as a member of the multi-disciplinary team responsible for assessing and developing policy relating to the total needs of the child. She will have a particular concern with the personal needs of the child and his family, including the maintenance of family links. . . the need to ensure that the well-being and needs of children in long-stay hospitals are adequately reviewed at appropriate intervals . ." (para.12:41)

"We consider that social workers who are concerned with sick children and their families should initially be familiar with the range of work associated with "child care" and not less skilled in this work than the former child care officers. From this base they would develop further expert knowledge in the needs of different groups of children and families or in the requirements of different settings. We have for example recommended the development of post qualification training in the field of child handicap." (para.20:31)

(3) The Committee pointed out the disquieting fact that many doctors at present working with children have very little understanding about child health, and in particular about the needs of handicapped children:

"Neither clinical medical officers nor general practitioners are required to have undergone any special training either in paediatrics or educational medicine before working in the school health service." (para.4:30)

"The standard of diagnosis, assessment, treatment and care for children suffering from physical, mental or multiple handicaps whether in the hospital or the community does not reach that largely achieved by the National Health Service for the treatment of acute illness." (para.14:12)

". . mental handicap specialists dealing with children have often had no training in either paediatrics or child psychiatry." (para.15:63)

"In our view, severely mentally handicapped children have more in common with other children because of their childhood than they have with severely mentally handicapped adults because of their common disability. . . Supporting services for them should therefore no longer be so sharply differentiated from those for more intelligent children, nor should they remain so predominantly the professional responsibility of specialists in mental subnormality." (para.14:76)

(4) The Committee recommended the creation of General Practitioner Paediatricians, Child-health Visitors, and Consultant Community Paediatricians. These new professional appointments, in some cases requiring special post-qualification training in paediatrics and child health, are envisaged not only as working closely with families, in clinics and in the paediatric departments of hospitals, but also in day and residential schools. If these recommendations are implemented, the child health services will be revitalised and far better integrated than ever before. With regard to children in long-stay hospitals, it is to be hoped that these child-oriented professionals would be empowered to visit their local long-stay hospitals and ensure that better services are available to the handicapped children living there, although

the Court Report did no actually spell out that they would take any responsibility for children in long-stay hospitals.

(5) *The Committee recommended the establishment of a District Handicap Team in every Health District.* The team would have a clinical and an operational function. The clinical function was listed as follows:

"i. to provide investigation and assessment of certain individual children with complex disorders and to arrange and co-ordinate their treatment;

ii. to provide their parents, teachers, child care staff, and others who may be directly concerned in their care, with the professional advice and support that can guide them in their management of the children;

iii. to encourage and assist professional field-work staff in their management and surveillance of these and other handicapped children locally, by being available for consultation either in the district child development centre or in local premises;

iv. to provide primary and supporting specialist services to special schools in the district." (para.14:23)

The operational functions of the team were listed as:

"i. to be involved with others at district and area level in epidemiological surveys of need; to monitor the effectiveness of the district service for handicapped children; to present data and suggestions for the development of the service; and to maintain the quality of its institutions;

ii. to act as source of information in the district about handicap in children and the services available;

iii. to organise seminars and courses of training for professional staff working in the district." (para.14:24)

Although the report did not delineate the actual responsibility the district handicap team should have for children in long-stay hospitals, it is to be hoped that the team will serve not only to prevent the unnecessary long-term admission of handicapped children to hospital, but will also monitor the services being received by these children who are already living in local long-stay hospitals.

(6) *The Committee referred to the need for an increase in all the therapy services (physiotherapists, speech therapists and occupational therapists),* and drew attention to the need for therapists to "examine the paediatric requirements of their discipline" (para.18.64). Perhaps as a result of the Court Report drawing the attention of therapists to their paediatric responsibilities, there may in future be an expansion of the therapy services for multiply handicapped children living in long-stay hospitals.

(7) *The Committee drew attention to the shortcomings in the supply and quality of aids and appliances for physically handicapped children.* It stated that "an efficient service can be justified on the simple ground of humanity"; and they recommended that "in future it should be a responsibility of each district handicap team to keep a constant watch on the supply of all aids and appliances to children in their district." (para.14:63)

154

Although the Court Report did not here refer specifically to the supply of aids and appliances to children in long-stay hospitals, it must be hoped that the brief of the district handicap team will include these children.

(8) The Committee recommended regular reviews of the needs of children in long-stay hospitals. It stated:

> "We believe that every child who is in hospital for more than three months should have a comprehensive review made of his service needs. This review should not be narrowly based but should extend to broader social and educational matters as well as to more strictly medical and/or psychiatric issues. It should, we believe, be carried out by a multi-disciplinary team drawn from an appropriately wide range of professional disciplines; it should particularly include those from the local authority who would be involved with the child at home or with his family. We think it will be found important to repeat these reviews at intervals, preferably every 6 months, and to consider where specific responsibility for the coordination of these reviews should rest bearing in mind that the involvement of local authority personnel is in our view essential." (para.16:15)

The above recommendation, if also followed by prompt action, would do much to alleviate the present neglect of children who live in long-stay hospitals.

(9) The Committee recommended that children's wards should be in the charge of a nurse with a qualification in nursing sick children (Registered Sick Children's Nurse).

> "In the hospital services, Senior Nursing Officers may cover a number of units and, with the relatively rare exceptions of the children's hospitals, seldom find themselves solely responsible for children. We recommend however that there should always be a senior nurse (of at least grade 8 of the Salmon scale) responsible for ensuring that children's needs are met and understood wherever there are children under hospital care, including inpatients (long-stay and short-stay), outpatients and day patients and that, even if this senior nurse has additional responsibilities not related to children, she should be a registered sick children's nurse." (para.21:30)

This recommendation may seem somewhat retrograde so far as long-stay hospital children are concerned, because these children are not necessarily sick children and they are more in need of a *home* than of nursing. However, there might be some definite advantages in the recommendation being implemented in mental handicap hospitals, in which the majority of senior nurses are qualified as registered nurses fo. the mentally subnormal or registered mental nurses, qualifications which are predominently geared to the care of mentally handicapped or mentally ill *adults*.

(10) The Committee drew attention to the need for teachers to act on their own initiative in relation to the total needs of the children they teach.

> "It is right and proper that teachers should exercise their own judgement in

seeking opinions of colleagues in other professions: and a necessary corollary is that they should be able to consult freely with these colleagues. Instead of hierarchical arrangements therefore, whereby all requests for advice from specialists in other services are made through a single, administrative channel, flexible arrangements are required which permit those in different disciplines to work on a "mini-team" basis, making a direct approach to colleagues as and when they see the need and taking independent action as they see fit. If this is to happen, all professional staff must assume responsibility for their actions and be accountable for them. They must also see that relevant information is passed to their colleagues in other disciplines." (para.14:21)

The above recommendation primarily referred to teachers in ordinary schools or in special schools, regarding the action they should take if they notice anything affecting the children they teach, for example the onset of a handicapping condition. However, all long-stay hospital school-teachers should also take note of this recommendation and interpret it as an exhortation to them to use their own judgement and *take action* if they are concerned about the care of the children in the hospital.

(11) The Court Report considers Joint Consultative Committees to be important in encouraging its recommendations. (Joint Consultative Committees are composed of officers and members of local authority councils and area health-authorities, and they were formed after the 1974 National Health Service reorganisation for the purpose of ensuring collaboration between Area Health Authorities and local councils regarding health and welfare matters.) The Court Report states:

"We see Joint Consultative Committees as an important forum from which to encourage local authority members to promote the recommendations in our report for better cooperation in child health . . . In this context they may wish to appoint a subcommittee of members of health and local authorities to advise on the development of services for children, including children who are mentally or physically handicapped." (para.21:5)

If Joint Consultative Committees do follow the Court Committee suggestion and appoint a subcommittee to oversee the local child-health services, the subcommittee should also give ample consideration to the needs of children in long-stay hospitals.

(12) The Committee referred to the important rôle of Community Health Councils in monitoring the services being received by various client groups.

"We believe it is of great importance that CHCs should investigate the needs of client groups in their districts and the extent to which those needs are being met. The least articulate are often the most disadvantaged members of the community and are therefore in greater need of a consumer voice to speak for them, for they are unable to speak for themselves. Such members include children in long-stay hospitals, mentally handicapped children,

156

mothers' with large families and low incomes, and immigrant families."
(para.21:35)

The sanguine expectations of the Court Committee as to the effectiveness of CHCs may eventually be realised, but hitherto these committees have shown little interest in the problems of children in long-stay hospitals, although many of their members were appointed ostensibly because of their interest in children.

(13) The Committee recommended the formation of a Joint Committee for Children to keep under constant review the needs of children and the services provided for them. This committee, operating at national level, might have responsibility for implementing the proposals of the Court Committee.

If the compassionate and child-oriented recommendations of the Court Committee are fully implemented, we should be on the way to achieving a just and efficient health service for all children, wherever they live, and whatever their needs might be. However, the successful implementation of the Committee's recommendations will depend very much on the willingness of professionals to accept changes for the sake of the children in their care.

It is appropriate to conclude with a final statement from the Court Report:

"It is our belief that children have special needs which they cannot articulate for themselves and that society has therefore a duty to ensure that these are identified and cogently represented." (para.16:19)

INDEX OF CHILDREN'S NAMES

RECOMMENDED FURTHER READING

Bayley, M. (1973) *Mental Handicap and Community Care.* London: Routledge and Kegan Paul.

Bowlby, J. (1951) *Maternal Care and Mental Health.* Geneva: W.H.O.

Burlingham, D., Freud, A. (1942) *Young Children in Wartime.* London: Allen and Unwin.

— — — — (1943) *Infants Without Families.* London: Allen and Unwin.

Children in Hospital in Wales: Final Report of the Working Party on Children in Hospital in Wales (1972). Welsh Hospital Board.

Clark, A. M., Clarke, A. D. B. (Eds.) (1974) *Mental Deficiency: the Changing Outlook,* 3rd. Edn. London: Methuen.

Cummings, P. (1973) *Education and the Severely Handicapped Child.* No. 6 in the series *Subnormality in the Seventies.* London: National Society for Mentally Handicapped Children.

Department of Health and Social Security (1969) *Report of the Committee of Enquiry into Allegations of Ill-treatment of Patients and Other Irregularities at the Ely Hospital, Cardiff.* Cmnd. 3795. London: H.M.S.O.

— — (1971) *Report of the Farleigh Committee of Enquiry.* Cmnd. 4557. London: H.M.S.O.

— — (1974) *Report of a Study Group on Mentally Handicapped Children in Residential Care.* (Chairman: D. E. Harvie) London: H.M.S.O.

— — (1974) *Report of the Committee of Enquiry into South Ockendon Hospital.* London: H.M.S.O.

Elvin, M., Santer-Westrate, H. (1974) 'Behaviour modification and activation therapy in a hospital for the SSN.' *Bulletin of the British Psychological Society,* **27,** 550-553.

Evidence to the Committee of Inquiry into Mental Handicap Nursing and Care (1976) given by the Health Care Evaluation Research Team (Director: Albert Kushlick, Dawn House, Sleepers Hill, Winchester).

Finnie, N. (1974) *Handling the Young Cerebral Palsied Child at Home,* 2nd Edn. London: William Heinemann Medical Books. (This book is by an experienced physiotherapist and gives excellent advice on the handling of young children with cerebral palsy.)

Goffman, E. (1961) *Asylums: Essays on the Social Situation of Mental Patients and Other Inmates.* New York: Doubleday.

Hall, D., Stacey, M. (Eds.) (1978) *Beyond Separation: Children in Hospital.* London: Routledge and Kegan Paul (in press).

Jones, K., Brown, J., Cunningham, W. J., Roberts, J., Williams, P. (1975) *Opening the Door: a Study of New Policies for the Mentally Handicapped.* London: Routledge and Kegan Paul.

King, R. D., Raynes, N. V., Tizard, J. (1971) *Patterns of Residential Care: Sociological Studies in Institutions for Handicapped Children.* London: Routledge and Kegan Paul.

Kugel, R. B., Wolfensberger, W. (Eds.) (1969) *Changing Patterns in Residential Services for the Mentally Retarded.* Report of the President's Panel on Mental Retardation. Washington, D.C.: U.S. Dept. of Health, Education and Welfare.

Kushlick, A. (1975) 'Some ways of staffing, monitoring and attaining objectives for services for disabled people.' *British Journal of Mental Subnormality,* **21,** 84-102.

Morris, P. (1969) *Put Away: a Sociological Study of Institutions for the Mentally Retarded.* London: Routledge and Kegan Paul.

Oswin, M. (1971) *The Empty Hours.* London: Allen Lane.

Shearer, A. (1974) 'Fostering mentally handicapped children: is it feasible?' London: Campaign for the Mentally Handicapped (96 Portland Place). Paper no. 3.

Tizard, B., Harvey, D. (Eds.) (1977) *Biology of Play.* Clinics in Developmental Medicine No. 62. London: S.I.M.P./Heinemann Medical.

Tizard, J. (1964) *Community Services for the Mentally Handicapped.* London: Oxford University Press.

— — Sinclair, I., Clark, R. V. G. (Eds.) (1975) *Varieties of Residential Experience.* London: Routledge and Kegan Paul.

159